50 French Cake Recipes for Home

By: Kelly Johnson

Table of Contents

- Tarte Tatin
- Gateau Basque
- Clafoutis
- Opera Cake
- Financier
- Fraisier
- Saint Honoré Cake
- Charlotte Russe
- Paris-Brest
- Kouign-Amann
- Gateau au Yaourt
- Buche de Noel
- Galette des Rois
- Pain d'Epices
- Gateau aux Pommes
- Cannelé
- Mille-Feuille
- Fondant au Chocolat
- Gateau Breton
- Moelleux au Chocolat
- Tarte aux Fraises
- Gateau de Savoie
- Gateau de Crepes
- Gateau aux Noix
- Tarte au Citron Meringuee
- Gateau Saint-Genix
- Gateau aux Carottes
- Pithivier
- Tarte Tropézienne
- Roulé à la Confiture
- Tarte aux Poires Bourdaloue
- Gateau à l'Orange
- Flognarde
- Tarte aux Pruneaux
- Gateau au Chocolat et aux Amandes

- Gateau Nantais
- Gateau au Fromage Blanc
- Tarte à la Rhubarbe
- Gateau aux Framboises
- Gateau au Citron
- Tarte aux Mirabelles
- Far Breton
- Gateau aux Marrons
- Tarte au Chocolat
- Quatre-Quarts
- Gateau au Miel
- Tarte aux Myrtilles
- Gateau aux Abricots
- Gateau au Beurre
- Tarte aux Figues

Tarte Tatin

Ingredients:

- 6-8 apples (Granny Smith or Golden Delicious)
- 1 cup granulated sugar
- 1/2 cup unsalted butter
- 1 sheet puff pastry
- Juice of 1 lemon
- 1 tsp vanilla extract

Instructions:

1. **Preheat the oven:**
   - Preheat your oven to 375°F (190°C).
2. **Prepare the apples:**
   - Peel, core, and quarter the apples. Toss them with lemon juice to prevent browning.
3. **Caramelize the sugar:**
   - In a heavy ovenproof skillet, melt the butter over medium heat. Add the sugar and cook until it dissolves and turns a light amber color, stirring occasionally to prevent burning.
4. **Arrange the apples:**
   - Remove the skillet from the heat and arrange the apple quarters tightly in the skillet, cut side up. Return the skillet to the stove and cook over medium heat for about 10 minutes, until the apples start to soften and the caramel thickens.
5. **Add the vanilla:**
   - Add the vanilla extract to the caramel and apples, stirring gently to combine.
6. **Prepare the puff pastry:**
   - Roll out the puff pastry on a lightly floured surface to fit the size of your skillet. Carefully place the puff pastry over the apples, tucking the edges down the sides of the skillet.
7. **Bake the tart:**
   - Place the skillet in the preheated oven and bake for 25-30 minutes, until the puff pastry is golden brown and puffed.
8. **Cool and invert:**
   - Remove the skillet from the oven and let the tart cool for a few minutes. Place a large plate or serving platter over the skillet and carefully invert the tart onto the plate.
9. **Serve:**
   - Serve the Tarte Tatin warm, optionally with a dollop of whipped cream or a scoop of vanilla ice cream.

Enjoy your delicious Tarte Tatin!

Gateau Basque

Ingredients:

- 2 cups all-purpose flour
- 1 tsp baking powder
- 1/2 tsp salt
- 3/4 cup unsalted butter, softened
- 3/4 cup granulated sugar
- 2 large eggs
- 1 tsp vanilla extract
- 1/4 tsp almond extract
- 1 cup pastry cream (store-bought or homemade)
- 1/2 cup cherry preserves

Instructions:

1. **Preheat the oven:**
    - Preheat your oven to 350°F (175°C). Grease a 9-inch round cake pan and line the bottom with parchment paper.
2. **Mix dry ingredients:**
    - In a medium bowl, whisk together the flour, baking powder, and salt.
3. **Cream butter and sugar:**
    - In a large mixing bowl, beat the softened butter and granulated sugar together until light and fluffy, about 2-3 minutes.
4. **Add eggs and extracts:**
    - Beat in the eggs, one at a time, until fully incorporated. Add the vanilla and almond extracts, mixing well.
5. **Combine wet and dry ingredients:**
    - Gradually add the dry ingredients to the butter mixture, mixing until just combined. The dough will be soft and slightly sticky.
6. **Divide the dough:**
    - Divide the dough into two equal portions. Press one portion into the bottom and up the sides of the prepared cake pan, forming an even layer.
7. **Add the filling:**
    - Spread the pastry cream evenly over the dough in the pan. Then, spread the cherry preserves over the pastry cream.
8. **Top with remaining dough:**
    - Roll out the second portion of dough on a lightly floured surface to fit the size of the cake pan. Carefully place it over the filling, sealing the edges with the dough from the sides.
9. **Bake the cake:**
    - Bake in the preheated oven for 35-40 minutes, until the top is golden brown and the edges are set.
10. **Cool and serve:**
    - Allow the Gateau Basque to cool in the pan for about 10 minutes before transferring it to a wire rack to cool completely. Serve at room temperature.

Enjoy your traditional Gateau Basque!

Clafoutis

Ingredients:

- 1 pound fresh cherries, pitted (or other fruit like berries or plums)
- 1/2 cup granulated sugar
- 1 cup whole milk
- 3 large eggs
- 1 tsp vanilla extract
- 1/2 cup all-purpose flour
- Pinch of salt
- Powdered sugar, for dusting (optional)

Instructions:

1. **Preheat the oven:**
   - Preheat your oven to 350°F (175°C). Grease a 9-inch pie dish or baking dish with butter.
2. **Prepare the fruit:**
   - If using cherries, pit them. If using other fruit, wash and slice as needed. Spread the fruit evenly in the prepared baking dish.
3. **Make the batter:**
   - In a medium bowl, whisk together the granulated sugar, eggs, and vanilla extract until well combined. Gradually add the flour and salt, whisking until smooth. Slowly pour in the milk, whisking continuously to avoid lumps. The batter should be smooth and slightly thick.
4. **Combine and bake:**
   - Pour the batter evenly over the fruit in the baking dish. The fruit may float to the top, which is normal.
5. **Bake the clafoutis:**
   - Place the baking dish in the preheated oven and bake for 35-40 minutes, or until the clafoutis is puffed, golden, and set in the center. A toothpick inserted into the center should come out clean.
6. **Cool and serve:**
   - Allow the clafoutis to cool slightly before dusting with powdered sugar, if desired. Serve warm or at room temperature.

Enjoy your delicious Clafoutis!

Opera Cake

Ingredients:

For the Joconde Sponge:

- 6 large eggs, separated
- 1/2 cup granulated sugar
- 2 cups almond flour
- 1/4 cup all-purpose flour
- 1/4 cup unsalted butter, melted

For the Coffee Syrup:

- 1/2 cup water
- 1/2 cup granulated sugar
- 1 tbsp instant coffee granules

For the Coffee Buttercream:

- 1 cup unsalted butter, softened
- 3/4 cup granulated sugar
- 1/4 cup water
- 5 large egg yolks
- 2 tbsp instant coffee granules dissolved in 1 tbsp hot water

For the Chocolate Ganache:

- 1 cup heavy cream
- 8 oz dark chocolate, finely chopped

For the Chocolate Glaze:

- 4 oz dark chocolate, finely chopped
- 1/4 cup unsalted butter

Instructions:

1. Make the Joconde Sponge:

1. Preheat the oven to 425°F (220°C). Line two 15x10-inch baking pans with parchment paper.
2. In a large bowl, whisk the egg whites until soft peaks form. Gradually add the sugar, continuing to whisk until stiff peaks form.
3. In another bowl, mix the almond flour and all-purpose flour. Add the egg yolks and melted butter, mixing until well combined.
4. Gently fold the egg white mixture into the almond mixture until just combined.
5. Spread the batter evenly into the prepared pans and bake for 5-7 minutes or until lightly golden. Let cool completely.

2. Prepare the Coffee Syrup:

1. In a small saucepan, combine the water, sugar, and coffee granules. Bring to a boil, then remove from heat and let cool.

3. Make the Coffee Buttercream:

1. In a small saucepan, combine the sugar and water. Bring to a boil and cook until the sugar syrup reaches 240°F (115°C).
2. In a mixing bowl, whisk the egg yolks until pale. Slowly pour the hot sugar syrup into the yolks while continuing to whisk until the mixture has cooled to room temperature.
3. Add the softened butter, a little at a time, whisking until smooth and creamy. Mix in the dissolved coffee.

4. Prepare the Chocolate Ganache:

1. Heat the cream in a small saucepan until it just begins to simmer. Pour over the chopped chocolate and let sit for a minute.
2. Stir until smooth and glossy. Let cool until it thickens to a spreadable consistency.

5. Assemble the Cake:

1. Cut the cooled Joconde sponge into three equal pieces to fit an 8x8-inch square cake pan.
2. Place the first sponge layer in the pan and brush generously with coffee syrup.
3. Spread half of the coffee buttercream over the sponge layer.
4. Add the second sponge layer, brush with coffee syrup, and spread with the chocolate ganache.
5. Add the final sponge layer, brush with coffee syrup, and spread the remaining coffee buttercream on top.
6. Chill the cake in the refrigerator for at least an hour.

6. Make the Chocolate Glaze:

1. Melt the chocolate and butter together until smooth. Let cool slightly.
2. Pour the glaze over the chilled cake, spreading it evenly to cover the top. Allow it to set in the refrigerator.

7. Serve:

1. Carefully remove the cake from the pan and trim the edges for a clean look.
2. Cut into slices and serve.

Financier

Ingredients:

- 1 cup (225g) unsalted butter
- 1 1/2 cups (150g) almond flour
- 1 1/2 cups (180g) powdered sugar
- 1/2 cup (60g) all-purpose flour
- 1/2 tsp salt
- 6 large egg whites
- 1 tsp vanilla extract
- Optional: Sliced almonds or fresh berries for topping

Instructions:

1. Prepare the Brown Butter:

1. In a small saucepan, melt the butter over medium heat.
2. Continue cooking, swirling the pan occasionally, until the butter turns golden brown and has a nutty aroma. This process should take about 5-7 minutes.
3. Remove from heat and let it cool slightly.

2. Preheat the Oven:

1. Preheat your oven to 375°F (190°C).
2. Grease a financier mold or a mini muffin tin with butter or non-stick spray.

3. Mix Dry Ingredients:

1. In a large bowl, sift together the almond flour, powdered sugar, all-purpose flour, and salt.

4. Whip the Egg Whites:

1. In a separate clean bowl, beat the egg whites until they become frothy. You don't need to whip them to stiff peaks, just until they are frothy.

5. Combine Ing

redients:

1. Gradually add the dry ingredients to the egg whites, folding gently until combined.
2. Add the slightly cooled brown butter and vanilla extract to the mixture, stirring until smooth.

6. Fill the Molds:

1. Pour the batter into the prepared molds, filling each about 3/4 full.
2. If desired, top each financier with a sliced almond or a fresh berry.

7. Bake:

1. Bake in the preheated oven for 12-15 minutes, or until the edges are golden brown and a toothpick inserted into the center comes out clean.
2. Remove from the oven and let them cool in the pan for a few minutes before transferring to a wire rack to cool completely.

8. Serve:

1. Serve the financiers warm or at room temperature. They are perfect with a cup of tea or coffee.

Fraisier

Ingredients:

For the Genoise Sponge:

- 4 large eggs
- 2/3 cup (130g) granulated sugar
- 1 cup (125g) all-purpose flour, sifted
- 1/4 cup (60g) unsalted butter, melted and cooled

For the Pastry Cream:

- 2 cups (500ml) whole milk
- 1 vanilla bean, split and seeds scraped (or 1 tsp vanilla extract)
- 5 large egg yolks
- 2/3 cup (130g) granulated sugar
- 1/4 cup (30g) cornstarch
- 2 tbsp (30g) unsalted butter

For the Syrup:

- 1/2 cup (100g) granulated sugar
- 1/2 cup (120ml) water
- 2 tbsp kirsch (optional)

For the Assembly:

- 1 1/2 pounds (700g) fresh strawberries, hulled and halved
- 1/2 cup (120ml) heavy cream, whipped to stiff peaks
- Marzipan or almond paste, for decoration (optional)
- Confectioners' sugar, for dusting

Instructions:

1. Make the Genoise Sponge:

1. Preheat your oven to 350°F (175°C). Grease and line a 9-inch (23cm) round cake pan with parchment paper.
2. In a heatproof bowl, whisk together the eggs and sugar. Place the bowl over a pot of simmering water and whisk continuously until the mixture is warm and the sugar is dissolved.
3. Remove from heat and continue to beat the mixture with an electric mixer until it triples in volume and forms a ribbon when the beaters are lifted.
4. Gently fold in the sifted flour, followed by the melted butter.
5. Pour the batter into the prepared pan and bake for 20-25 minutes, or until the cake is golden brown and a toothpick inserted into the center comes out clean.
6. Let the cake cool in the pan for 10 minutes, then transfer to a wire rack to cool completely.

2. Make the Pastry Cream:

1. In a saucepan, heat the milk and vanilla bean (or extract) over medium heat until just boiling. Remove from heat and let it infuse.
2. In a bowl, whisk together the egg yolks, sugar, and cornstarch until smooth.
3. Gradually pour the hot milk into the egg mixture, whisking constantly to prevent curdling.
4. Return the mixture to the saucepan and cook over medium heat, whisking constantly, until the mixture thickens and boils.
5. Remove from heat and stir in the butter until smooth.
6. Pour the pastry cream into a bowl, cover with plastic wrap (pressing it directly onto the surface to prevent a skin from forming), and refrigerate until cool.

3. Make the Syrup:

1. In a small saucepan, combine the sugar and water. Bring to a boil, stirring until the sugar is dissolved.
2. Remove from heat and stir in the kirsch (if using). Let cool.

4. Assemble the Fraisier:

1. Slice the cooled genoise sponge in half horizontally to create two layers.
2. Place one layer in the bottom of a 9-inch (23cm) springform pan or cake ring.
3. Brush the layer with half of the syrup.
4. Arrange the halved strawberries around the edge of the pan, cut side facing out. Fill the center with more strawberries.
5. Fold the whipped cream into the cooled pastry cream and spread half of this mixture over the strawberries and sponge layer.
6. Place the second layer of sponge on top, brush with the remaining syrup, and spread the rest of the pastry cream mixture over the top.
7. Smooth the top with a spatula and refrigerate for at least 4 hours or overnight to set.

5. Decorate:

1. If using marzipan or almond paste, roll it out thinly and cut a circle to fit the top of the cake.
2. Place the marzipan on top of the set pastry cream.
3. Dust with confectioners' sugar before serving.

6. Serve:

1. Carefully remove the springform pan or cake ring.
2. Slice and serve the Fraisier, enjoying the combination of fresh strawberries, creamy filling, and light sponge.

Saint Honoré Cake

Ingredients:

For the Puff Pastry Base:

- 1 sheet puff pastry, thawed

For the Choux Pastry (Pâte à Choux):

- 1/2 cup (120ml) water
- 1/2 cup (120ml) milk
- 1/2 cup (115g) unsalted butter
- 1 tbsp sugar
- 1/4 tsp salt
- 1 cup (125g) all-purpose flour
- 4 large eggs

For the Pastry Cream:

- 2 cups (500ml) whole milk
- 1 vanilla bean, split and seeds scraped (or 1 tsp vanilla extract)
- 5 large egg yolks
- 2/3 cup (130g) granulated sugar
- 1/4 cup (30g) cornstarch
- 2 tbsp (30g) unsalted butter

For the Caramel:

- 1 cup (200g) granulated sugar
- 1/4 cup (60ml) water

For the Whipped Cream:

- 1 cup (240ml) heavy cream
- 2 tbsp powdered sugar
- 1 tsp vanilla extract

Instructions:

1. Prepare the Puff Pastry Base:

1. Preheat your oven to 375°F (190°C).
2. Roll out the puff pastry sheet and cut out a 9-inch (23cm) circle. Place it on a parchment-lined baking sheet.
3. Prick the pastry with a fork to prevent it from puffing too much during baking.
4. Bake for 15-20 minutes, or until golden brown. Remove from oven and let cool completely.

2. Make the Choux Pastry:

1. Preheat your oven to 425°F (220°C). Line a baking sheet with parchment paper.
2. In a medium saucepan, combine water, milk, butter, sugar, and salt. Bring to a boil over medium heat.
3. Add flour all at once and stir vigorously until the mixture forms a ball and pulls away from the sides of the pan.
4. Remove from heat and let cool slightly.
5. Add eggs one at a time, beating well after each addition until the dough is smooth and glossy.
6. Transfer the dough to a piping bag fitted with a large round tip.
7. Pipe small rounds (about 1 inch in diameter) onto the prepared baking sheet.
8. Bake for 10 minutes at 425°F (220°C), then reduce the temperature to 350°F (175°C) and bake for an additional 20 minutes, or until the choux pastries are golden brown and crisp. Let cool completely.

3. Prepare the Pastry Cream:

1. In a saucepan, heat the milk and vanilla bean (or extract) over medium heat until just boiling. Remove from heat and let it infuse.
2. In a bowl, whisk together the egg yolks, sugar, and cornstarch until smooth.
3. Gradually pour the hot milk into the egg mixture, whisking constantly to prevent curdling.
4. Return the mixture to the saucepan and cook over medium heat, whisking constantly, until the mixture thickens and boils.
5. Remove from heat and stir in the butter until smooth.
6. Pour the pastry cream into a bowl, cover with plastic wrap (pressing it directly onto the surface to prevent a skin from forming), and refrigerate until cool.

4. Make the Caramel:

1. In a medium saucepan, combine the sugar and water. Heat over medium heat, swirling the pan occasionally, until the sugar dissolves and the mixture turns a deep amber color.
2. Remove from heat immediately to prevent burning.

5. Make the Whipped Cream:

1. In a large mixing bowl, beat the heavy cream, powdered sugar, and vanilla extract until stiff peaks form.
2. Transfer the whipped cream to a piping bag fitted with a star tip.

6. Assemble the Saint Honoré Cake:

1. Place the puff pastry base on a serving platter.
2. Fill another piping bag with pastry cream and fill the choux pastries.
3. Dip the tops of the filled choux pastries into the caramel and place them around the edge of the puff pastry base, sticking them together with a bit of caramel.
4. Spread a layer of pastry cream over the puff pastry base.
5. Pipe a generous amount of whipped cream in a decorative pattern on top of the pastry cream.
6. Arrange more choux pastries on top if desired, and finish with a drizzle of caramel.

7. Serve:

1. Carefully slice and serve the Saint Honoré Cake, enjoying the combination of crisp choux, creamy filling, and rich caramel.

Charlotte Russe

Ingredients:

For the Ladyfingers:

- 4 large eggs, separated
- 1/2 cup (100g) granulated sugar
- 1/2 tsp vanilla extract
- 1/2 cup (60g) all-purpose flour
- Powdered sugar, for dusting

For the Filling:

- 2 cups (480ml) heavy cream
- 1/2 cup (100g) granulated sugar
- 1 tbsp gelatin powder
- 1/4 cup (60ml) cold water
- 2 tsp vanilla extract
- Fresh berries or fruit, for garnish (optional)

Instructions:

1. Prepare the Ladyfingers:

1. Preheat your oven to 350°F (175°C). Line two baking sheets with parchment paper.
2. In a large bowl, beat the egg yolks and 1/4 cup (50g) of the sugar until thick and pale. Stir in the vanilla extract.
3. In another bowl, whisk the egg whites until soft peaks form. Gradually add the remaining 1/4 cup (50g) sugar and continue to whisk until stiff peaks form.
4. Gently fold the egg whites into the egg yolk mixture.
5. Sift the flour over the mixture and fold gently until just combined.
6. Transfer the batter to a piping bag fitted with a plain round tip.
7. Pipe ladyfingers (about 3 inches long) onto the prepared baking sheets, spacing them about 1 inch apart.
8. Dust the ladyfingers with powdered sugar.
9. Bake for 10-12 minutes, or until lightly golden and set. Remove from oven and let cool completely on the baking sheets.

2. Prepare the Filling:

1. In a small bowl, sprinkle the gelatin over the cold water and let it bloom for about 5 minutes.
2. In a saucepan, heat 1/2 cup (120ml) of the heavy cream until just boiling. Remove from heat and add the bloomed gelatin, stirring until completely dissolved. Let it cool to room temperature.
3. In a large mixing bowl, beat the remaining 1 1/2 cups (360ml) heavy cream with the granulated sugar and vanilla extract until soft peaks form.
4. Gradually add the gelatin mixture to the whipped cream, beating until stiff peaks form.

3. Assemble the Charlotte Russe:

1. Line the sides of an 8-inch (20cm) springform pan or a charlotte mold with parchment paper.
2. Arrange the ladyfingers vertically around the sides of the pan, with the sugared side facing out. Place more ladyfingers on the bottom of the pan to form the base.
3. Pour the whipped cream mixture into the pan, spreading it evenly.
4. Cover the top with more ladyfingers, if desired.
5. Refrigerate the charlotte for at least 4 hours, or until set.

4. Serve:

1. Carefully remove the charlotte from the pan and transfer it to a serving plate.
2. Garnish with fresh berries or fruit, if desired.
3. Slice and serve, enjoying the light and creamy filling with the delicate ladyfingers.

Enjoy your elegant and delicious Charlotte Russe!

Paris-Brest

Ingredients:

For the Choux Pastry:

- 1 cup (240ml) water
- 1/2 cup (115g) unsalted butter
- 1/4 tsp salt
- 1 cup (125g) all-purpose flour
- 4 large eggs

For the Praline Cream:

- 1 cup (240ml) whole milk
- 1/2 cup (100g) granulated sugar
- 4 large egg yolks
- 1/4 cup (30g) cornstarch
- 1/2 cup (115g) unsalted butter, softened
- 1/2 cup (125g) praline paste (or hazelnut paste)

For Assembly:

- Powdered sugar, for dusting
- Sliced almonds, toasted (optional)

Instructions:

1. Prepare the Choux Pastry:

1. Preheat your oven to 400°F (200°C). Line a baking sheet with parchment paper and draw a 9-inch (23cm) circle on it as a guide.
2. In a medium saucepan, combine the water, butter, and salt. Bring to a boil over medium heat.
3. Add the flour all at once and stir vigorously with a wooden spoon until the mixture forms a ball and pulls away from the sides of the pan.
4. Remove from heat and let it cool for a few minutes.
5. Add the eggs one at a time, beating well after each addition until the dough is smooth and glossy.
6. Transfer the dough to a piping bag fitted with a large plain tip.
7. Pipe a ring of dough onto the parchment paper, following the circle guide. Pipe a second ring inside the first one, touching it. Pipe a third ring on top of the first two rings, forming a crown.
8. Bake in the preheated oven for 25-30 minutes, or until the pastry is golden brown and puffed. Turn off the oven and leave the door ajar to let the pastry dry out for another 10 minutes.
9. Remove from the oven and let cool completely on a wire rack.

2. Prepare the Praline Cream:

1. In a medium saucepan, heat the milk until it begins to steam, but do not let it boil.
2. In a bowl, whisk together the sugar, egg yolks, and cornstarch until smooth and pale.
3. Gradually pour the hot milk into the egg mixture, whisking constantly to prevent curdling.

4. Return the mixture to the saucepan and cook over medium heat, whisking constantly, until it thickens and comes to a boil. Continue to cook for 1-2 minutes.
5. Remove from heat and stir in the praline paste until smooth.
6. Transfer the mixture to a bowl, cover with plastic wrap touching the surface, and let it cool to room temperature.
7. Once cooled, beat the softened butter into the praline pastry cream until light and fluffy.

3. Assemble the Paris-Brest:

1. Carefully slice the cooled choux pastry ring horizontally with a serrated knife.
2. Pipe or spread the praline cream generously onto the bottom half of the pastry ring.
3. Place the top half of the pastry ring over the cream, pressing down gently.
4. Dust the top with powdered sugar and sprinkle with toasted sliced almonds if desired.

4. Serve:

1. Slice the Paris-Brest into portions and serve.

Enjoy your delicious and creamy Paris-Brest, a classic French dessert!

Kouign-Amann

Ingredients:

- 2 cups (250g) all-purpose flour
- 1/2 cup (120ml) warm water
- 1/2 cup (120ml) warm milk
- 2 tsp (7g) active dry yeast
- 1/2 tsp salt
- 1 tbsp (12g) granulated sugar
- 1 cup (225g) unsalted butter, cold
- 1 cup (200g) granulated sugar, for sprinkling
- Extra butter and sugar for the muffin tin

Instructions:

1. Prepare the Dough:

1. In a large mixing bowl, combine the warm water, warm milk, and active dry yeast. Stir gently and let it sit for 5-10 minutes until frothy.
2. Add the flour, salt, and 1 tablespoon of sugar to the yeast mixture. Mix until a dough forms.
3. Knead the dough on a lightly floured surface for about 5-7 minutes until smooth and elastic.
4. Place the dough in a lightly greased bowl, cover with a damp cloth, and let it rise in a warm place for about 1 hour, or until doubled in size.

2. Prepare the Butter:

1. While the dough is rising, place the cold butter between two sheets of parchment paper.
2. Using a rolling pin, pound and roll the butter into a rectangle about 5x8 inches (12x20 cm) and 1/4 inch (0.6 cm) thick.
3. Place the butter rectangle in the refrigerator to keep it cold.

3. Laminate the Dough:

1. Once the dough has risen, punch it down to release the air. Roll it out on a lightly floured surface into a rectangle about 8x12 inches (20x30 cm).
2. Place the cold butter rectangle in the center of the dough. Fold the dough over the butter, encasing it completely. Seal the edges by pinching them together.
3. Roll out the dough into a large rectangle, approximately 8x16 inches (20x40 cm).
4. Fold the dough into thirds, like a letter, and then rotate it 90 degrees. Roll it out again into a large rectangle and fold into thirds once more.
5. Wrap the dough in plastic wrap and refrigerate for 30 minutes.

4. Shape and Bake:

1. Preheat your oven to 400°F (200°C). Generously butter and sugar a muffin tin.
2. Roll out the chilled dough into a large rectangle, about 12x16 inches (30x40 cm).
3. Sprinkle the entire surface with the granulated sugar.
4. Fold the dough into thirds, then roll it out again to its original size. Sprinkle with more sugar, and repeat the folding and rolling process one more time.

5. Cut the dough into 12 squares.
6. Take each square and fold the corners towards the center, pinching them together to form a round shape. Place each piece into a muffin cup.
7. Sprinkle the tops with additional sugar.

5. Bake:

1. Bake the Kouign-Amann in the preheated oven for 25-30 minutes, or until golden brown and caramelized.
2. Allow them to cool in the muffin tin for a few minutes before transferring to a wire rack to cool completely.

Enjoy your delightful, buttery, and caramelized Kouign-Amann!

Gateau au Yaourt

Ingredients:

- 1 cup (125g) plain yogurt
- 1 cup (200g) granulated sugar
- 1/2 cup (120ml) vegetable oil
- 2 cups (250g) all-purpose flour
- 1 1/2 tsp baking powder
- 1/2 tsp baking soda
- 1/4 tsp salt
- 2 large eggs
- 1 tsp vanilla extract
- Zest of 1 lemon (optional)

Instructions:

1. Prepare the Oven and Pan:

1. Preheat your oven to 350°F (180°C). Grease a 9-inch (23 cm) round cake pan and line the bottom with parchment paper.

2. Mix the Wet Ingredients:

1. In a large mixing bowl, whisk together the yogurt, sugar, and vegetable oil until well combined.
2. Add the eggs one at a time, beating well after each addition.
3. Stir in the vanilla extract and lemon zest (if using).

3. Combine the Dry Ingredients:

1. In a separate bowl, sift together the flour, baking powder, baking soda, and salt.

4. Combine Wet and Dry Ingredients:

1. Gradually add the dry ingredients to the wet ingredients, mixing until just combined. Do not overmix; it's okay if there are a few lumps.

5. Bake the Cake:

1. Pour the batter into the prepared cake pan and smooth the top with a spatula.
2. Bake in the preheated oven for 30-35 minutes, or until a toothpick inserted into the center of the cake comes out clean.
3. Allow the cake to cool in the pan for 10 minutes, then transfer it to a wire rack to cool completely.

6. Serve:

1. Once the cake has cooled, you can dust it with powdered sugar or serve it plain. It's also delicious with a dollop of whipped cream or a drizzle of fruit syrup.

Enjoy your moist and flavorful Gâteau au Yaourt, a classic French yogurt cake that's simple to make and perfect for any occasion!

Buche de Noel

Ingredients:

For the Sponge Cake:

- 4 large eggs, separated
- 1/2 cup (100g) granulated sugar, divided
- 1 tsp vanilla extract
- 1/2 cup (60g) all-purpose flour
- 1/4 cup (25g) unsweetened cocoa powder
- 1/2 tsp baking powder
- 1/4 tsp salt

For the Filling:

- 1 cup (240ml) heavy cream
- 2 tbsp powdered sugar
- 1 tsp vanilla extract

For the Chocolate Ganache:

- 1 cup (240ml) heavy cream
- 8 oz (225g) bittersweet chocolate, finely chopped

For Decoration:

- Powdered sugar (for dusting)
- Fresh berries, holly leaves, or other festive decorations

Instructions:

1. Prepare the Sponge Cake:

1. Preheat your oven to 350°F (175°C). Grease a 15x10-inch (38x25 cm) jelly roll pan and line it with parchment paper.
2. In a large mixing bowl, beat the egg yolks with 1/4 cup (50g) of granulated sugar until thick and pale. Stir in the vanilla extract.
3. In a separate bowl, sift together the flour, cocoa powder, baking powder, and salt.
4. In another large bowl, beat the egg whites until soft peaks form. Gradually add the remaining 1/4 cup (50g) of granulated sugar and continue beating until stiff peaks form.
5. Gently fold the flour mixture into the egg yolk mixture until just combined. Then, carefully fold in the beaten egg whites until no white streaks remain.
6. Spread the batter evenly into the prepared jelly roll pan. Bake for 10-12 minutes, or until the cake springs back when lightly touched.

2. Roll the Cake:

1. While the cake is baking, lay a clean kitchen towel on a flat surface and dust it generously with powdered sugar.

2. As soon as the cake is done, carefully invert it onto the prepared towel. Peel off the parchment paper and roll the cake up in the towel, starting from one of the short sides. Allow it to cool completely in this rolled-up position.

3. Prepare the Filling:

1. In a mixing bowl, beat the heavy cream, powdered sugar, and vanilla extract until stiff peaks form.

4. Fill and Roll the Cake:

1. Once the cake has cooled, carefully unroll it. Spread the whipped cream evenly over the cake, leaving a small border around the edges.
2. Gently re-roll the cake (without the towel) and place it seam-side down on a serving platter.

5. Prepare the Chocolate Ganache:

1. In a small saucepan, heat the heavy cream over medium heat until it begins to simmer.
2. Remove from heat and add the chopped chocolate, stirring until completely melted and smooth. Allow the ganache to cool slightly until it thickens to a spreadable consistency.

6. Frost the Cake:

1. Spread the chocolate ganache evenly over the rolled cake, covering it completely. Use a fork to create a bark-like texture on the ganache.

7. Decorate:

1. Dust the cake lightly with powdered sugar to resemble snow. Add fresh berries, holly leaves, or other festive decorations as desired.

Enjoy your beautiful and delicious Bûche de Noël, a classic French Yule log cake perfect for the holiday season!

Galette des Rois

Ingredients:

- 2 sheets of puff pastry (about 9-10 inches / 23-25 cm in diameter)
- 1 cup (100g) almond flour or finely ground almonds
- 1/2 cup (100g) granulated sugar
- 1/2 cup (115g) unsalted butter, softened
- 2 large eggs
- 1 tsp almond extract
- 1 dry bean or small figurine (to hide inside the galette)
- Powdered sugar, for dusting

Instructions:

1. Prepare the Almond Filling:

1. In a mixing bowl, cream together the softened butter and sugar until light and fluffy.
2. Add the almond flour (or ground almonds), eggs, and almond extract. Mix until well combined and smooth. Set aside.

2. Assemble the Galette:

1. Preheat your oven to 375°F (190°C).
2. Place one sheet of puff pastry on a baking sheet lined with parchment paper.
3. Spread the almond filling evenly over the puff pastry sheet, leaving a small border around the edges.
4. If desired, place a dry bean or small figurine somewhere in the almond filling (traditionally to symbolize the King or Queen).
5. Brush the edges of the pastry with water to help seal the galette.
6. Place the second sheet of puff pastry on top of the filling. Press the edges firmly to seal, and trim any excess pastry if necessary. You can crimp the edges with a fork for a decorative touch.

3. Bake the Galette:

1. Using a sharp knife, lightly score the top of the galette in a crosshatch pattern (be careful not to cut all the way through).
2. Brush the top of the galette with a little water or beaten egg for a golden finish.
3. Bake in the preheated oven for 25-30 minutes, or until the galette is golden brown and puffed up.

4. Serve:

1. Allow the galette to cool slightly before serving. Traditionally, it is served warm or at room temperature.
2. Before serving, dust the galette with powdered sugar for a decorative finish.
3. Cut into slices and enjoy your Galette des Rois, a delicious French pastry traditionally enjoyed during Epiphany celebrations!

Pain d'Epices

Ingredients:

- 1 cup (240ml) water
- 1 cup (340g) honey
- 1 cup (200g) brown sugar
- 2 1/2 cups (320g) all-purpose flour
- 1 tsp baking powder
- 1 tsp baking soda
- 2 tsp ground cinnamon
- 1 tsp ground ginger
- 1/2 tsp ground cloves
- 1/2 tsp ground nutmeg
- Zest of 1 orange
- Zest of 1 lemon

Instructions:

1. Prepare the Batter:

1. In a saucepan, combine water, honey, and brown sugar. Heat over medium heat, stirring occasionally, until the mixture comes to a boil. Remove from heat and let it cool slightly.
2. Preheat your oven to 350°F (175°C). Grease and flour a loaf pan.
3. In a large mixing bowl, sift together the flour, baking powder, baking soda, cinnamon, ginger, cloves, and nutmeg.
4. Gradually add the honey mixture to the dry ingredients, stirring until well combined.
5. Stir in the orange zest and lemon zest until evenly distributed.

2. Bake the Pain d'Épices:

1. Pour the batter into the prepared loaf pan, spreading it evenly.
2. Bake in the preheated oven for 50-60 minutes, or until a toothpick inserted into the center comes out clean.
3. Remove from the oven and let the pain d'épices cool in the pan for 10 minutes. Then, transfer it to a wire rack to cool completely.

3. Serve:

1. Once cooled, slice and serve the pain d'épices on its own or with butter, cheese, or jam.
2. Enjoy this traditional French spiced bread, perfect for breakfast or as a snack with tea or coffee!

Gateau aux Pommes

Ingredients:

- 3 large apples (such as Granny Smith), peeled, cored, and sliced
- 1 tbsp lemon juice
- 1 cup (200g) granulated sugar
- 1/2 cup (120ml) vegetable oil
- 2 large eggs
- 1 tsp vanilla extract
- 1 1/2 cups (190g) all-purpose flour
- 1 1/2 tsp baking powder
- 1/4 tsp salt
- 1/2 cup (120ml) milk
- Powdered sugar, for dusting (optional)

Instructions:

1. Prepare the Apples:

1. Preheat your oven to 350°F (175°C). Grease and flour a 9-inch (23cm) round cake pan.
2. In a bowl, toss the sliced apples with lemon juice to prevent browning. Set aside.

2. Prepare the Batter:

1. In a large mixing bowl, whisk together the sugar, vegetable oil, eggs, and vanilla extract until smooth.
2. In a separate bowl, sift together the flour, baking powder, and salt.
3. Gradually add the dry ingredients to the wet ingredients, alternating with the milk, beginning and ending with the flour mixture. Mix until just combined.

3. Assemble the Cake:

1. Pour half of the batter into the prepared cake pan and spread it evenly.
2. Arrange half of the sliced apples over the batter in an even layer.
3. Pour the remaining batter over the apples and spread it evenly.
4. Arrange the remaining sliced apples over the top of the cake, pressing them slightly into the batter.

4. Bake the Cake:

1. Bake in the preheated oven for 45-55 minutes, or until a toothpick inserted into the center of the cake comes out clean.
2. Remove the cake from the oven and let it cool in the pan for about 10 minutes.
3. Transfer the cake to a wire rack to cool completely.

5. Serve:

1. Once cooled, dust the gâteau aux pommes with powdered sugar if desired.
2. Slice and serve the cake as a delightful dessert or snack with tea or coffee.

Enjoy this classic French apple cake, showcasing the natural sweetness of apples in a moist and delicious treat!

Cannelé

Ingredients:

- 2 cups (500ml) whole milk
- 2 tbsp (30g) unsalted butter
- 1 cup (200g) granulated sugar
- 1 vanilla bean (or 1 tsp vanilla extract)
- 1/2 cup (65g) all-purpose flour
- 2 large eggs
- 2 large egg yolks
- 1/4 cup (60ml) dark rum
- Butter or baking spray, for greasing

Instructions:

1. Prepare the Batter:

1. In a saucepan, combine the milk, butter, and sugar over medium heat. Split the vanilla bean lengthwise and scrape out the seeds into the milk mixture. Add the vanilla bean pod as well. Heat until the mixture comes to a simmer, stirring occasionally to dissolve the sugar. Remove from heat and let it cool slightly.
2. In a mixing bowl, whisk together the flour, eggs, and egg yolks until smooth.
3. Gradually pour the warm milk mixture into the flour mixture, whisking constantly until well combined and smooth.
4. Stir in the dark rum. Cover the bowl with plastic wrap and refrigerate for at least 24 hours (up to 48 hours). This resting period allows the flavors to develop and ensures the proper texture.

2. Prepare the Molds:

1. Preheat your oven to 450°F (230°C). Generously butter or spray cannelé molds with baking spray.
2. Place the greased molds on a baking sheet and place in the oven for about 5 minutes to preheat.

3. Bake the Cannelés:

1. Remove the molds from the oven and pour the chilled batter into the hot molds, filling them almost to the top.
2. Place the molds back into the oven and immediately reduce the temperature to 375°F (190°C).
3. Bake for 50-60 minutes, or until the cannelés are dark brown and caramelized on the outside, and set but slightly custardy on the inside.

4. Cool and Serve:

1. Remove the cannelés from the molds while they are still warm. Use a knife or silicone spatula to gently release them.
2. Let the cannelés cool on a wire rack. They are best enjoyed slightly warm or at room temperature.

5. Optional Step:

1. Dust the cannelés with powdered sugar before serving for an added touch of sweetness.

Enjoy these classic French pastries, with their caramelized exteriors and soft, custardy centers, perfect with coffee or tea!

Mille-Feuille

Ingredients:

- 1 sheet of puff pastry (store-bought or homemade)
- 1 cup (240ml) whole milk
- 3 egg yolks
- 1/4 cup (50g) granulated sugar
- 2 tbsp cornstarch
- 1 tsp vanilla extract
- 1 cup (240ml) heavy cream
- 2 tbsp powdered sugar
- Fresh berries or fruit (optional, for garnish)
- Confectioners' sugar, for dusting

Instructions:

1. Prepare the Pastry:

1. Preheat your oven to 400°F (200°C). Line a baking sheet with parchment paper.
2. Roll out the puff pastry sheet on a lightly floured surface to about 1/4 inch thickness. Transfer the pastry to the prepared baking sheet. Prick the pastry all over with a fork to prevent it from puffing up too much.
3. Bake the pastry in the preheated oven for 15-20 minutes, or until golden brown and puffed. Remove from oven and let cool completely on a wire rack.

2. Prepare the Pastry Cream:

1. In a medium saucepan, heat the milk over medium heat until steaming but not boiling.
2. In a mixing bowl, whisk together the egg yolks, sugar, and cornstarch until pale and creamy.
3. Gradually pour the hot milk into the egg yolk mixture, whisking constantly to temper the eggs.
4. Return the mixture to the saucepan and cook over medium heat, stirring constantly with a wooden spoon or whisk, until the mixture thickens and comes to a boil.
5. Remove from heat and stir in the vanilla extract. Transfer the pastry cream to a bowl and cover with plastic wrap, pressing the wrap directly onto the surface of the cream to prevent a skin from forming. Refrigerate until chilled and firm, about 2 hours.

3. Prepare the Whipped Cream:

1. In a mixing bowl, whip the heavy cream and powdered sugar together until stiff peaks form.

4. Assemble the Mille-Feuille:

1. Once the pastry and pastry cream are cooled, cut the pastry sheet into three equal rectangular pieces.
2. Place one piece of pastry on a serving platter. Spread a layer of pastry cream evenly over the pastry.
3. Place a second piece of pastry on top of the cream layer and press gently to adhere. Spread another layer of pastry cream over this piece.

4. Finally, place the third piece of pastry on top of the second cream layer. Lightly dust the top with confectioners' sugar.
5. Pipe or spread the whipped cream over the top layer of pastry.
6. Garnish with fresh berries or fruit if desired.

5. Serve:

1. Refrigerate the assembled mille-feuille for at least 1 hour before serving to allow the flavors to meld.
2. Slice with a sharp knife and serve chilled. Enjoy this classic French dessert with its layers of delicate pastry and creamy filling!

This recipe yields a delicious mille-feuille that's perfect for special occasions or elegant desserts.

Fondant au Chocolat

Ingredients:

- 7 oz (200g) dark chocolate (60-70% cocoa), chopped
- 1/2 cup (115g) unsalted butter, plus extra for greasing
- 3/4 cup (150g) granulated sugar
- 3 large eggs
- 1/2 cup (60g) all-purpose flour
- Cocoa powder or powdered sugar, for dusting (optional)

Instructions:

1. Prepare the Chocolate Mixture:

1. Preheat your oven to 350°F (175°C). Grease individual ramekins or a muffin tin with butter and dust with cocoa powder or powdered sugar.
2. In a heatproof bowl set over a pan of simmering water (double boiler method), melt the chopped chocolate and butter together, stirring occasionally until smooth. Remove from heat and let cool slightly.

2. Prepare the Batter:

1. In a mixing bowl, whisk together the sugar and eggs until pale and creamy.
2. Gradually pour the melted chocolate mixture into the egg mixture, whisking constantly until well combined.
3. Fold in the flour gently until just incorporated. Be careful not to overmix.

3. Bake the Fondants:

1. Divide the batter evenly among the prepared ramekins or muffin tin.
2. Place in the preheated oven and bake for about 12-15 minutes (for ramekins) or 10-12 minutes (for muffin tin), or until the tops are set but the centers still jiggle slightly.
3. Remove from the oven and let cool in the ramekins or tin for a few minutes.

4. Serve:

1. Carefully run a knife around the edges of each fondant to loosen it from the ramekin or muffin tin.
2. Invert the fondants onto serving plates. Dust with cocoa powder or powdered sugar if desired.
3. Serve immediately while warm, with a scoop of vanilla ice cream or whipped cream on the side, if desired.

4. Enjoy:

1. These fondants are best enjoyed warm, just after baking, when the centers are still molten. The rich, gooey chocolate center paired with the slightly firm outer layer makes for a decadent dessert experience.

Gateau Breton

Ingredients:

- 2 cups (250g) all-purpose flour
- 1 cup (200g) granulated sugar
- 1 cup (230g) unsalted butter, softened
- 4 large egg yolks
- 1/4 tsp salt
- 1 tbsp rum (optional)
- Egg wash (1 egg yolk mixed with 1 tbsp water), for brushing

Instructions:

1. Prepare the Dough:

1. In a large mixing bowl, cream together the softened butter and sugar until light and fluffy.
2. Add the egg yolks one at a time, mixing well after each addition.
3. Stir in the rum (if using).
4. Gradually add the flour and salt, mixing until the dough comes together and forms a cohesive ball. It will be a soft, slightly crumbly dough.
5. Shape the dough into a disk, wrap it in plastic wrap, and refrigerate for at least 1 hour (or overnight) to chill and firm up.

2. Preheat the Oven:

1. Preheat your oven to 350°F (175°C). Line a baking sheet with parchment paper.

3. Shape and Bake the Gateau Breton:

1. Once chilled, divide the dough into two equal portions.
2. On a lightly floured surface, roll out one portion of the dough into a circle or square about 1/2 inch (1.5 cm) thick.
3. Transfer the rolled dough to the prepared baking sheet.
4. Use a fork to prick the surface of the dough all over to create a decorative pattern and to prevent it from puffing up too much during baking.
5. Brush the surface of the dough with the egg wash.
6. Optionally, use a knife to create a crisscross pattern on the top.
7. Repeat the same process with the second portion of dough.

4. Bake:

1. Bake the gateaux in the preheated oven for 25-30 minutes, or until golden brown and cooked through. The edges should be slightly darker.
2. Remove from the oven and let cool on a wire rack.

5. Serve:

1. Once completely cooled, slice the Gateau Breton into wedges or squares.

2. Enjoy this rich and buttery Breton cake with a cup of tea or coffee. It's perfect for dessert or as a treat any time of day.

Notes:

- Gateau Breton can be stored in an airtight container at room temperature for several days. It also freezes well for longer storage.
- You can customize this cake by adding raisins, nuts, or citrus zest to the dough for additional flavor variations.

Moelleux au Chocolat

Ingredients:

- 7 oz (200g) dark chocolate (60-70% cocoa), chopped
- 1/2 cup (115g) unsalted butter, plus extra for greasing
- 1/2 cup (100g) granulated sugar
- 3 large eggs
- 1/4 cup (30g) all-purpose flour
- Cocoa powder or powdered sugar, for dusting (optional)
- Berries or whipped cream, for serving (optional)

Instructions:

1. Prepare the Chocolate Mixture:

1. Preheat your oven to 350°F (175°C). Grease individual ramekins or muffin tin cups with butter and dust with cocoa powder or powdered sugar.
2. In a heatproof bowl set over a pan of simmering water (double boiler method), melt the chopped chocolate and butter together, stirring occasionally until smooth. Remove from heat and let cool slightly.

2. Prepare the Batter:

1. In a mixing bowl, whisk together the sugar and eggs until pale and creamy.
2. Gradually pour the melted chocolate mixture into the egg mixture, whisking constantly until well combined.
3. Fold in the flour gently until just incorporated. Be careful not to overmix.

3. Bake the Moelleux au Chocolat:

1. Divide the batter evenly among the prepared ramekins or muffin tin cups.
2. Place in the preheated oven and bake for about 10-12 minutes (for ramekins) or 8-10 minutes (for muffin tin), or until the tops are set but the centers still jiggle slightly.
3. Remove from the oven and let cool in the ramekins or tin for a few minutes.

4. Serve:

1. Carefully run a knife around the edges of each moelleux to loosen it from the ramekin or muffin tin.
2. Invert the moelleux onto serving plates. Dust with cocoa powder or powdered sugar if desired.
3. Serve immediately while warm, accompanied by berries or a dollop of whipped cream, if desired.

5. Enjoy:

1. Moelleux au Chocolat is best enjoyed warm, just after baking, when the centers are still molten and the exterior is slightly firm. It's a decadent dessert that melts in your mouth with every bite.

Tarte aux Fraises

Ingredients:

For the Pastry:

- 1 1/4 cups (150g) all-purpose flour
- 1/4 cup (30g) almond flour (or finely ground almonds)
- 1/2 cup (113g) unsalted butter, cold and cut into cubes
- 1/4 cup (50g) granulated sugar
- 1/4 tsp salt
- 1 large egg yolk
- 1-2 tbsp cold water, if needed

For the Filling:

- 1 lb (450g) fresh strawberries, hulled and halved (reserve some whole for decoration)
- 1/2 cup (120ml) strawberry jam or preserves
- 1 tbsp lemon juice
- Fresh mint leaves, for garnish (optional)
- Powdered sugar, for dusting (optional)

Instructions:

1. Make the Pastry:

1. In a food processor, combine the all-purpose flour, almond flour, sugar, and salt. Pulse briefly to mix.
2. Add the cold butter cubes and pulse until the mixture resembles coarse breadcrumbs.
3. Add the egg yolk and pulse again until the dough starts to come together. If necessary, add cold water, 1 tablespoon at a time, until the dough forms a ball.
4. Turn out the dough onto a lightly floured surface and knead briefly until smooth. Flatten into a disc, wrap in plastic wrap, and refrigerate for at least 30 minutes.

2. Preheat the Oven:

1. Preheat your oven to 375°F (190°C).
2. On a lightly floured surface, roll out the chilled pastry dough into a circle about 1/8 inch (3mm) thick.
3. Carefully transfer the dough to a 9-inch (23cm) tart pan with a removable bottom. Press the dough into the edges and trim any excess. Prick the bottom of the dough with a fork to prevent it from puffing up during baking.

3. Blind Bake the Pastry:

1. Line the pastry with parchment paper or aluminum foil and fill with pie weights, dried beans, or rice.
2. Bake in the preheated oven for about 15 minutes. Remove the parchment paper and weights and bake for an additional 5-7 minutes, or until the crust is golden brown.
3. Remove from the oven and let cool completely on a wire rack.

4. Prepare the Filling:

1. In a small saucepan, heat the strawberry jam or preserves with the lemon juice over low heat until melted and smooth. Remove from heat and let cool slightly.
2. Arrange the halved strawberries in the cooled tart shell, cut side down, in a circular pattern, filling the entire tart shell.
3. Brush the melted jam mixture over the strawberries to glaze them evenly.

5. Serve:

1. Garnish with fresh mint leaves, if desired, and dust with powdered sugar.
2. Slice and serve the tart at room temperature. Enjoy this delightful French dessert with its fresh, fruity flavors!

Notes:

- You can customize this tart by adding a layer of pastry cream or whipped cream before arranging the strawberries for added richness.
- Store any leftover tart in the refrigerator, covered, and consume within a day or two for the best taste and texture.

Gateau de Savoie

Ingredients:

- 4 large eggs, separated
- 1/2 cup (100g) granulated sugar
- 1/2 cup (65g) cake flour
- 1/4 cup (30g) cornstarch
- 1/2 tsp vanilla extract
- Zest of 1 lemon (optional)
- Pinch of salt
- Powdered sugar, for dusting

Instructions:

1. Preheat Oven and Prepare Pan:

1. Preheat your oven to 350°F (175°C). Grease and flour a 9-inch (23cm) round cake pan.

2. Beat Egg Yolks and Sugar:

1. In a large mixing bowl, beat the egg yolks and sugar together until pale and creamy. Add the vanilla extract and lemon zest (if using), and mix well.

3. Add Dry Ingredients:

1. Sift the cake flour and cornstarch together. Gradually fold the flour mixture into the egg yolk mixture until well combined.

4. Beat Egg Whites:

1. In a separate clean bowl, beat the egg whites with a pinch of salt until stiff peaks form.

5. Combine Batter:

1. Gently fold one-third of the beaten egg whites into the batter to lighten it.
2. Carefully fold in the remaining egg whites, being careful not to deflate the mixture.

6. Bake the Cake:

1. Pour the batter into the prepared cake pan and smooth the top with a spatula.
2. Bake in the preheated oven for 25-30 minutes, or until the cake is golden brown and a toothpick inserted into the center comes out clean.

7. Cool and Serve:

1. Remove the cake from the oven and let it cool in the pan for about 10 minutes.
2. Carefully invert the cake onto a wire rack to cool completely.

8. Dust with Powdered Sugar:

1. Once cooled, transfer the cake to a serving platter and dust with powdered sugar before serving.

9. Serve:

1. Slice and serve the Gateau de Savoie on its own or with fresh berries and whipped cream for a delightful French dessert experience.

Notes:

- Gateau de Savoie is known for its light and airy texture, making it perfect for pairing with fruits or a light custard.
- Store any leftovers in an airtight container at room temperature for up to 2 days.

Gateau de Crepes

Ingredients:

For the Crêpes:

- 1 cup (125g) all-purpose flour
- 2 tbsp granulated sugar
- 1/4 tsp salt
- 3 large eggs
- 1 1/2 cups (360ml) milk
- 2 tbsp unsalted butter, melted
- 1 tsp vanilla extract
- Butter or oil for cooking crêpes

For the Filling:

- 2 cups (480ml) heavy cream
- 1/4 cup (30g) powdered sugar
- 1 tsp vanilla extract
- Fresh berries or fruit preserves for layering

Optional Garnish:

- Powdered sugar
- Fresh berries

Instructions:

1. Make the Crêpe Batter:

1. In a large mixing bowl, whisk together the flour, sugar, and salt.
2. In another bowl, whisk together the eggs, milk, melted butter, and vanilla extract.
3. Gradually pour the wet ingredients into the dry ingredients, whisking until smooth and no lumps remain. The batter should be thin and pourable.
4. Let the batter rest for at least 30 minutes at room temperature, or refrigerate for up to 24 hours.

2. Cook the Crêpes:

1. Heat a non-stick skillet or crêpe pan over medium heat. Brush with butter or oil.
2. Pour about 1/4 cup of batter into the pan, swirling to coat the bottom evenly. Cook for about 1-2 minutes, until the edges start to lift and the bottom is golden brown.
3. Flip the crêpe and cook for another 1-2 minutes, until golden brown. Transfer to a plate and repeat with the remaining batter, stacking the cooked crêpes on top of each other. You should have about 20-25 crêpes.

3. Make the Filling:

1. In a large mixing bowl, beat the heavy cream, powdered sugar, and vanilla extract until stiff peaks form.

4. Assemble the Crêpe Cake:

1. Place one crêpe on a serving plate or cake stand. Spread a thin layer of whipped cream over the crêpe.
2. Continue layering crêpes and whipped cream, alternating each layer. Optional: add fresh berries or fruit preserves between some layers for extra flavor.
3. Finish with a crêpe on top. Refrigerate the cake for at least 1 hour before serving to allow the layers to set.

5. Garnish and Serve:

1. Dust the top of the crêpe cake with powdered sugar.
2. Garnish with fresh berries or fruit, if desired.
3. Slice and serve the Gateau de Crêpes chilled. Enjoy this delightful and elegant French dessert!

Notes:

- The crêpe cake can be assembled ahead of time and refrigerated for up to 24 hours before serving.
- Experiment with different fillings such as chocolate ganache, lemon curd, or Nutella for variation.
- Adjust the sweetness of the filling according to your taste preferences.

Gateau aux Noix

Ingredients:

- 1 cup (120g) walnuts, finely ground
- 1 cup (125g) all-purpose flour
- 1 tsp baking powder
- 1/2 tsp baking soda
- 1/4 tsp salt
- 1/2 cup (115g) unsalted butter, softened
- 1 cup (200g) granulated sugar
- 3 large eggs
- 1 tsp vanilla extract
- 1/2 cup (120ml) plain yogurt or sour cream
- Powdered sugar, for dusting (optional)

Instructions:

1. Prepare the Walnuts:

1. Preheat your oven to 350°F (175°C). Grease and flour a 9-inch (23cm) round cake pan.
2. In a food processor or blender, finely grind the walnuts until they resemble coarse crumbs. Be careful not to over-process into walnut butter.

2. Mix Dry Ingredients:

1. In a bowl, whisk together the ground walnuts, flour, baking powder, baking soda, and salt until well combined. Set aside.

3. Cream Butter and Sugar:

1. In a large mixing bowl, cream together the softened butter and granulated sugar until light and fluffy.

4. Add Eggs and Vanilla:

1. Beat in the eggs, one at a time, until well incorporated. Add the vanilla extract and mix well.

5. Combine Wet and Dry Ingredients:

1. Gradually add the flour mixture to the butter mixture, alternating with the plain yogurt or sour cream, beginning and ending with the flour mixture. Mix until just combined. Do not overmix.

6. Bake the Cake:

1. Pour the batter into the prepared cake pan and smooth the top with a spatula.
2. Bake in the preheated oven for 30-35 minutes, or until a toothpick inserted into the center comes out clean.

7. Cool and Serve:

1. Remove the cake from the oven and let it cool in the pan for about 10 minutes.
2. Carefully invert the cake onto a wire rack to cool completely.

8. Dust with Powdered Sugar (Optional):

1. Once cooled, transfer the cake to a serving platter and dust with powdered sugar before serving.

9. Serve:

1. Slice and serve the Gateau aux Noix on its own or with a dollop of whipped cream or a scoop of vanilla ice cream for a delightful dessert.

Notes:

- You can toast the walnuts lightly before grinding for added flavor.
- Store any leftovers in an airtight container at room temperature for up to 3 days, or freeze for longer storage.

Tarte au Citron Meringuee

Ingredients:

For the Crust:

- 1 1/4 cups (150g) all-purpose flour
- 1/4 cup (50g) granulated sugar
- 1/2 cup (115g) unsalted butter, cold and cut into small cubes
- 1/4 tsp salt
- 1 large egg yolk
- 1-2 tbsp ice water, if needed

For the Lemon Filling:

- 1 cup (200g) granulated sugar
- 3 tbsp cornstarch
- 1/4 tsp salt
- 1 cup (240ml) water
- 1/2 cup (120ml) freshly squeezed lemon juice (about 3-4 lemons)
- 2 tbsp lemon zest
- 4 large egg yolks
- 2 tbsp unsalted butter

For the Meringue:

- 4 large egg whites, at room temperature
- 1/2 cup (100g) granulated sugar
- 1/4 tsp cream of tartar

Instructions:

1. Prepare the Crust:

1. In a food processor, pulse together the flour, sugar, and salt until combined.
2. Add the cold cubed butter and pulse until the mixture resembles coarse crumbs.
3. Add the egg yolk and pulse until the dough starts to come together. If needed, add 1-2 tablespoons of ice water, a little at a time, until the dough forms a ball.
4. Flatten the dough into a disk, wrap it in plastic wrap, and refrigerate for at least 30 minutes.
5. Preheat your oven to 375°F (190°C). Roll out the chilled dough on a lightly floured surface to fit a 9-inch (23cm) tart pan. Press the dough into the bottom and sides of the pan, trimming any excess. Prick the bottom of the crust with a fork.
6. Line the crust with parchment paper or aluminum foil, and fill it with pie weights or dried beans.
7. Bake the crust for 15 minutes. Remove the weights and parchment/foil, then bake for an additional 10-12 minutes, or until the crust is golden brown. Let it cool completely.

2. Make the Lemon Filling:

1. In a medium saucepan, whisk together the sugar, cornstarch, and salt.
2. Gradually whisk in the water, lemon juice, and lemon zest until smooth.

3. Place the saucepan over medium heat and cook, stirring constantly, until the mixture thickens and comes to a boil.
4. Remove from heat. In a small bowl, whisk the egg yolks. Gradually whisk in about half of the hot lemon mixture to temper the eggs.
5. Return the tempered egg mixture to the saucepan with the remaining lemon mixture. Cook over medium heat, stirring constantly, until thickened, about 2-3 minutes.
6. Remove from heat and stir in the butter until melted and smooth.
7. Pour the lemon filling into the cooled tart crust, spreading it evenly. Set aside while you make the meringue.

3. Make the Meringue:

1. In a clean, dry mixing bowl, beat the egg whites on medium speed until foamy.
2. Add the cream of tartar and continue beating until soft peaks form.
3. Gradually add the granulated sugar, a spoonful at a time, while beating on high speed, until stiff, glossy peaks form.

4. Assemble and Bake the Tart:

1. Preheat your oven to 350°F (175°C).
2. Spread the meringue over the hot lemon filling, starting at the edges to seal to the crust. Use the back of a spoon to create swirls or peaks.
3. Bake the tart for 10-12 minutes, or until the meringue is lightly golden brown.
4. Remove from the oven and let the tart cool completely on a wire rack.

5. Chill and Serve:

1. Once cooled, refrigerate the tart for at least 2 hours, or until the filling is set.
2. Slice and serve the Tarte au Citron Meringuée chilled. Enjoy this classic French dessert with its tangy lemon filling and fluffy meringue topping!

Notes:

- Store any leftovers in the refrigerator, covered, for up to 3 days.
- For best results, use fresh lemon juice and zest for a vibrant flavor in the filling.

Gateau Saint-Genix

Ingredients:

For the Brioche Dough:

- 2 cups (250g) all-purpose flour
- 1/4 cup (50g) granulated sugar
- 1/2 tsp salt
- 1 tbsp active dry yeast
- 1/2 cup (120ml) warm milk
- 2 large eggs
- 1/2 cup (115g) unsalted butter, softened

For the Praline Paste:

- 1 cup (100g) almonds, blanched and peeled
- 1/2 cup (100g) granulated sugar
- 1 tbsp water

For the Gâteau Saint-Genix:

- Brioche dough
- Praline paste
- 1/2 cup (75g) red candied cherries
- 1/4 cup (40g) pearl sugar (optional, for decoration)

Instructions:

1. Make the Brioche Dough:

1. In a small bowl, dissolve the yeast and 1 tablespoon of sugar in warm milk. Let it sit for about 5-10 minutes until frothy.
2. In a large bowl or the bowl of a stand mixer fitted with the dough hook, combine the flour, remaining sugar, and salt.
3. Add the activated yeast mixture and eggs to the flour mixture. Mix until combined.
4. Gradually add the softened butter, a few pieces at a time, kneading until the dough is smooth and elastic. This may take about 10-15 minutes by hand or 8-10 minutes with a stand mixer.
5. Cover the dough with a clean kitchen towel and let it rise in a warm place for about 1-2 hours, or until doubled in size.

2. Prepare the Praline Paste:

1. In a skillet or pan, toast the blanched almonds over medium heat until lightly golden and fragrant. Remove from heat and let them cool.
2. In a saucepan, combine the sugar and water over medium-high heat. Stir until the sugar dissolves, then bring to a boil without stirring.
3. Continue boiling until the mixture reaches a golden amber color (about 10-12 minutes).
4. Remove from heat and immediately stir in the toasted almonds. Stir vigorously to coat the almonds evenly with caramel.

5. Transfer the praline mixture to a baking sheet lined with parchment paper. Let it cool completely, then break it into pieces and grind it into a fine paste in a food processor.

3. Assemble the Gâteau Saint-Genix:

1. Preheat your oven to 350°F (180°C). Grease a Gâteau Saint-Genix mold or a standard round cake pan.
2. Punch down the risen brioche dough and knead it briefly on a lightly floured surface.
3. Roll out the dough into a rectangle about 1/2 inch thick.
4. Spread the praline paste evenly over the dough, leaving a border around the edges.
5. Scatter the red candied cherries evenly over the praline paste.
6. Roll the dough tightly from one long end to the other, creating a log shape.
7. Cut the log into slices about 1 inch thick.
8. Arrange the slices in the prepared mold or cake pan, pressing them lightly together. Let them rise for another 30 minutes.
9. Sprinkle pearl sugar over the top of the dough slices if desired.

4. Bake and Serve:

1. Bake the Gâteau Saint-Genix in the preheated oven for 25-30 minutes, or until golden brown and cooked through.
2. Remove from the oven and let it cool slightly before serving.
3. Serve warm or at room temperature. Enjoy this delicious French pastry with its unique praline and cherry filling!

Notes:

- Gâteau Saint-Genix is traditionally made in a special mold that gives it its characteristic shape, but you can use a standard cake pan as well.
- The praline paste can be prepared in advance and stored in an airtight container at room temperature until ready to use.

Gateau aux Carottes

Ingredients:

For the Cake:

- 2 cups (250g) all-purpose flour
- 2 tsp baking powder
- 1 tsp baking soda
- 1/2 tsp salt
- 1 tsp ground cinnamon
- 1/2 tsp ground nutmeg
- 1/2 tsp ground ginger
- 1 cup (200g) granulated sugar
- 1 cup (240ml) vegetable oil
- 4 large eggs
- 2 cups (250g) grated carrots (about 3-4 medium carrots)
- 1/2 cup (50g) chopped walnuts or pecans (optional)
- Zest of 1 orange (optional)

For the Cream Cheese Frosting:

- 8 oz (225g) cream cheese, softened
- 1/2 cup (115g) unsalted butter, softened
- 2 cups (250g) powdered sugar, sifted
- 1 tsp vanilla extract

Instructions:

1. Prepare the Cake:

1. Preheat your oven to 350°F (175°C). Grease and flour a 9-inch (23cm) round cake pan or line it with parchment paper.
2. In a medium bowl, whisk together the flour, baking powder, baking soda, salt, cinnamon, nutmeg, and ginger until well combined. Set aside.
3. In a large bowl, whisk together the granulated sugar and vegetable oil until smooth and combined.
4. Add the eggs one at a time, whisking well after each addition.
5. Gradually add the dry flour mixture to the wet ingredients, mixing until just combined.
6. Fold in the grated carrots, chopped nuts (if using), and orange zest (if using) until evenly distributed throughout the batter.
7. Pour the batter into the prepared cake pan, spreading it evenly.
8. Bake for 30-35 minutes, or until a toothpick inserted into the center of the cake comes out clean.
9. Remove the cake from the oven and let it cool in the pan for 10 minutes before transferring it to a wire rack to cool completely.

2. Make the Cream Cheese Frosting:

1. In a large bowl, beat the softened cream cheese and butter together until smooth and creamy.

2. Gradually add the powdered sugar, beating well after each addition, until the frosting is smooth and fluffy.
3. Stir in the vanilla extract until well combined.

3. Assemble the Cake:

1. Once the cake has cooled completely, spread a generous layer of cream cheese frosting over the top of the cake.
2. Optionally, garnish with additional chopped nuts or orange zest for decoration.
3. Slice and serve the Gâteau aux Carottes. Enjoy this delicious French-style carrot cake with its rich, creamy frosting!

Notes:

- Make sure the cream cheese and butter are both softened to room temperature for smooth frosting.
- You can adjust the sweetness of the frosting by adding more or less powdered sugar, according to your taste.
- Store any leftovers in an airtight container in the refrigerator for up to 3-4 days.

Pithivier

Ingredients:

For the Pastry:

- 2 sheets of puff pastry (store-bought or homemade), thawed if frozen

For the Almond Cream (Frangipane):

- 1/2 cup (115g) unsalted butter, softened
- 1/2 cup (100g) granulated sugar
- 1 cup (100g) almond flour (ground almonds)
- 2 large eggs
- 1 tsp almond extract
- 1 tbsp all-purpose flour
- Zest of 1 lemon (optional)

For Assembly:

- 1 egg, beaten (for egg wash)
- Powdered sugar, for dusting

Instructions:

1. Prepare the Almond Cream (Frangipane):

1. In a mixing bowl, cream together the softened butter and granulated sugar until light and fluffy.
2. Add the almond flour and mix until well combined.
3. Beat in the eggs, one at a time, ensuring each is fully incorporated before adding the next.
4. Mix in the almond extract and lemon zest (if using).
5. Finally, fold in the all-purpose flour until the mixture is smooth and homogeneous. Set aside.

2. Prepare the Pithivier:

1. Preheat your oven to 400°F (200°C). Line a baking sheet with parchment paper.
2. Roll out one sheet of puff pastry on a lightly floured surface into a circle of about 10-12 inches (25-30 cm) in diameter, depending on the desired size of your Pithivier.
3. Spread the prepared almond cream (frangipane) evenly over the center of the pastry circle, leaving a border of about 1 inch (2.5 cm) around the edge.
4. Brush the edges of the pastry with beaten egg.
5. Roll out the second sheet of puff pastry to a similar size and place it carefully over the almond cream-covered pastry circle.
6. Press down gently around the edges to seal the two pastry sheets together.
7. Using a sharp knife, trim the edges to create a neat, round shape. You can also crimp the edges with a fork for decoration.
8. Brush the top of the Pithivier with beaten egg for a shiny finish.
9. With a sharp knife, lightly score the top of the Pithivier in a decorative pattern (such as a crisscross or spiral).

3. Bake the Pithivier:

1. Place the assembled Pithivier onto the prepared baking sheet.
2. Bake in the preheated oven for 25-30 minutes, or until the pastry is golden brown and puffed up.
3. Remove from the oven and let it cool on a wire rack for at least 15-20 minutes before serving.

4. Serve:

1. Once cooled slightly, dust the Pithivier with powdered sugar for a decorative finish.
2. Slice and serve warm or at room temperature. Enjoy the delicious, flaky layers filled with almond cream!

Notes:

- Pithivier can be served as a dessert or a sweet pastry for tea or coffee.
- You can customize the filling by adding sliced fruits or other flavors to the almond cream if desired.
- Store any leftovers in an airtight container at room temperature for up to 2 days, or refrigerate for longer freshness. Reheat gently in the oven before serving if desired.

Tarte Tropézienne

Ingredients:

For the Brioche Dough:

- 2 cups (250g) all-purpose flour
- 1/4 cup (50g) granulated sugar
- 1 tsp active dry yeast
- 1/2 tsp salt
- 3 large eggs, at room temperature
- 1/4 cup (60ml) warm milk
- 1/2 cup (115g) unsalted butter, softened

For the Pastry Cream:

- 1 cup (240ml) whole milk
- 3 large egg yolks
- 1/4 cup (50g) granulated sugar
- 2 tbsp cornstarch
- 1 tsp vanilla extract
- Zest of 1 lemon

For the Sugar Syrup:

- 1/4 cup (50g) granulated sugar
- 1/4 cup (60ml) water
- 1 tbsp orange blossom water (optional)

For Assembly:

- Confectioners' sugar, for dusting
- 1 cup (240ml) heavy cream
- 1 tbsp confectioners' sugar
- 1 tsp vanilla extract

Instructions:

1. Prepare the Brioche Dough:

1. In a large mixing bowl, combine the flour, sugar, yeast, and salt. Make a well in the center.
2. In a separate bowl, whisk together the eggs and warm milk.
3. Pour the egg mixture into the well of the dry ingredients and stir until combined.
4. Add the softened butter and knead the dough until smooth and elastic, about 10-15 minutes by hand or 5-7 minutes with a stand mixer fitted with a dough hook.
5. Cover the dough with plastic wrap and let it rise in a warm place until doubled in size, about 1-2 hours.
6. Punch down the dough and divide it into two equal portions. Shape each portion into a ball and place them on a baking sheet lined with parchment paper. Cover loosely with plastic wrap and let them rise again for about 1 hour.

7. Preheat your oven to 375°F (190°C).
8. Bake the brioche balls for 15-20 minutes or until golden brown. Remove from the oven and let them cool completely on a wire rack.

2. Prepare the Pastry Cream:

1. In a saucepan, heat the milk over medium heat until it just begins to simmer. Remove from heat.
2. In a mixing bowl, whisk together the egg yolks, sugar, and cornstarch until pale and creamy.
3. Slowly pour the hot milk into the egg mixture, whisking constantly to temper the eggs.
4. Return the mixture to the saucepan and cook over medium heat, stirring constantly, until thickened and smooth. This should take about 5-7 minutes.
5. Remove from heat and stir in the vanilla extract and lemon zest.
6. Transfer the pastry cream to a bowl and cover the surface with plastic wrap to prevent a skin from forming. Chill in the refrigerator until completely cold.

3. Prepare the Sugar Syrup:

1. In a small saucepan, combine the sugar and water. Bring to a boil over medium heat, stirring until the sugar has dissolved.
2. Remove from heat and stir in the orange blossom water, if using. Let the syrup cool completely.

4. Assemble the Tarte Tropézienne:

1. Once the brioche balls and pastry cream are cooled, carefully slice each brioche ball horizontally into two equal layers.
2. Brush the cut sides of each brioche layer generously with the prepared sugar syrup.
3. In a mixing bowl, whip the heavy cream with confectioners' sugar and vanilla extract until stiff peaks form.
4. Spread a thick layer of pastry cream over the bottom half of one brioche layer.
5. Gently place the top half of the brioche layer over the pastry cream, pressing down lightly.
6. Spread the whipped cream over the top of the assembled Tarte Tropézienne.
7. Dust with confectioners' sugar for decoration.
8. Refrigerate the Tarte Tropézienne for at least 2 hours before serving to allow the flavors to meld.

9. Serve:

1. Slice the Tarte Tropézienne into wedges and serve chilled or at room temperature.
2. Enjoy the delightful combination of fluffy brioche, creamy pastry cream, and whipped cream in every bite!

Roulé à la Confiture

Ingredients:

For the Sponge Cake:

- 4 large eggs
- 1/2 cup (100g) granulated sugar
- 1/2 cup (60g) all-purpose flour
- 1/2 tsp baking powder
- 1/4 tsp salt
- 1 tsp vanilla extract

For Filling:

- 1 cup (250g) fruit jam or preserves (such as raspberry, strawberry, or apricot)
- Powdered sugar, for dusting

Instructions:

1. Prepare the Sponge Cake:

1. Preheat your oven to 350°F (180°C). Grease a 10x15 inch (25x38 cm) jelly roll pan or baking sheet, then line it with parchment paper. Grease the parchment paper as well.
2. In a large mixing bowl, beat the eggs and granulated sugar with an electric mixer on high speed until the mixture is thick and pale yellow, about 5-7 minutes.
3. Add the vanilla extract and mix until combined.
4. In a separate bowl, sift together the flour, baking powder, and salt.
5. Gently fold the flour mixture into the egg mixture using a spatula, taking care not to deflate the batter.
6. Pour the batter into the prepared pan, spreading it evenly with a spatula to ensure it reaches all corners.
7. Bake for 10-12 minutes, or until the top is lightly golden and the cake springs back when lightly pressed with your finger.
8. While the cake is baking, lay out a clean kitchen towel and dust it generously with powdered sugar.
9. Once baked, immediately invert the hot cake onto the prepared towel. Carefully peel off the parchment paper.
10. Starting from one of the shorter ends, gently roll the cake and the towel together into a log shape. Place seam-side down on a wire rack to cool completely.

2. Assemble the Roulé à la Confiture:

1. Carefully unroll the cooled cake from the towel.
2. Spread the fruit jam or preserves evenly over the surface of the cake, leaving a small border around the edges.
3. Starting from the same shorter end, gently roll the cake back up into a log shape, using the towel to help guide you. Place seam-side down on a serving platter.
4. Dust the top of the cake with powdered sugar for a decorative finish.
5. Chill the Roulé à la Confiture in the refrigerator for at least 30 minutes to allow the filling to set.

6. Serve:

1. Slice the Roulé à la Confiture into rounds and serve chilled or at room temperature.
2. Enjoy this classic French dessert with its light sponge and fruity filling, perfect for any occasion!

Tarte aux Poires Bourdaloue

Ingredients:

For the Tart Dough:

- 1 1/4 cups (150g) all-purpose flour
- 1/2 cup (100g) granulated sugar
- 1/4 tsp salt
- 1/2 cup (115g) unsalted butter, cold and cut into small cubes
- 1 large egg yolk
- 1-2 tbsp cold water

For the Almond Cream (Frangipane):

- 1/2 cup (115g) unsalted butter, softened
- 1/2 cup (100g) granulated sugar
- 1 cup (100g) almond flour or finely ground almonds
- 2 large eggs
- 1 tsp vanilla extract

For the Poached Pears:

- 3-4 ripe pears, peeled, halved, and cored
- 1/2 lemon
- 1/2 cup (100g) granulated sugar
- 1 cup (240ml) water
- 1 cinnamon stick (optional)

For Assembly:

- 2 tbsp apricot jam, melted (for glaze)
- Slivered almonds, for garnish (optional)

Instructions:

1. Prepare the Tart Dough:

1. In a food processor, combine the flour, sugar, and salt. Pulse a few times to mix.
2. Add the cold cubed butter and pulse until the mixture resembles coarse crumbs.
3. Add the egg yolk and 1 tablespoon of cold water. Pulse until the dough comes together. If needed, add more water, 1 teaspoon at a time, until the dough forms a ball.
4. Turn the dough out onto a lightly floured surface and gently knead it into a smooth ball. Flatten into a disk, wrap in plastic wrap, and refrigerate for at least 1 hour.

2. Prepare the Almond Cream (Frangipane):

1. In a mixing bowl, cream together the softened butter and sugar until light and fluffy.
2. Add the almond flour and mix until well combined.
3. Beat in the eggs, one at a time, mixing well after each addition.

4. Stir in the vanilla extract. Set aside.

3. Prepare the Poached Pears:

1. In a large saucepan, squeeze the lemon juice into the water. Add the sugar and cinnamon stick (if using). Stir over medium heat until the sugar dissolves.
2. Add the pear halves to the saucepan, making sure they are submerged in the poaching liquid.
3. Simmer gently for about 15-20 minutes, or until the pears are tender when pierced with a knife.
4. Remove the pears from the poaching liquid and let them cool slightly. Cut each pear half into thin slices.

4. Assemble the Tarte aux Poires Bourdaloue:

1. Preheat your oven to 375°F (190°C). Grease a 9-inch (23 cm) tart pan with removable bottom.
2. On a lightly floured surface, roll out the chilled tart dough into a circle about 1/8 inch (3 mm) thick. Carefully transfer the dough to the prepared tart pan, pressing it gently into the bottom and up the sides. Trim any excess dough.
3. Spread the almond cream (frangipane) evenly over the bottom of the tart shell.
4. Arrange the pear slices in a decorative pattern over the almond cream.
5. Bake the tart in the preheated oven for 35-40 minutes, or until the almond cream is set and the crust is golden brown.
6. Remove the tart from the oven and let it cool on a wire rack.

5. Finish:

1. Brush the melted apricot jam over the top of the warm tart to glaze.
2. Sprinkle with slivered almonds, if desired, for garnish.
3. Serve the Tarte aux Poires Bourdaloue warm or at room temperature. Enjoy this classic French tart with its delicate almond cream and tender poached pears!

Gateau à l'Orange

Ingredients:

For the Cake:

- 1 1/2 cups (180g) all-purpose flour
- 1 1/2 tsp baking powder
- 1/4 tsp salt
- 1 cup (200g) granulated sugar
- Zest of 2 oranges
- 1/2 cup (120ml) fresh orange juice (from about 2 oranges)
- 1/2 cup (120ml) vegetable oil or melted butter
- 3 large eggs
- 1/2 cup (120ml) plain yogurt or sour cream
- 1 tsp vanilla extract

For the Orange Syrup:

- 1/2 cup (120ml) fresh orange juice
- 1/4 cup (50g) granulated sugar

For the Orange Glaze:

- 1 cup (120g) powdered sugar
- 2-3 tbsp fresh orange juice
- Zest of 1 orange (optional, for garnish)

Instructions:

1. Prepare the Cake:

1. Preheat your oven to 350°F (175°C). Grease and flour a 9-inch (23cm) round cake pan or line it with parchment paper.
2. In a medium bowl, whisk together the flour, baking powder, and salt. Set aside.
3. In a large bowl, combine the sugar and orange zest. Rub the zest into the sugar with your fingers to release the oils and flavor.
4. Add the orange juice, oil (or melted butter), eggs, yogurt (or sour cream), and vanilla extract to the sugar mixture. Whisk until smooth and well combined.
5. Gradually add the dry ingredients to the wet ingredients, whisking until the batter is smooth and no lumps remain.
6. Pour the batter into the prepared cake pan and smooth the top with a spatula.
7. Bake in the preheated oven for 30-35 minutes, or until a toothpick inserted into the center of the cake comes out clean.

2. Prepare the Orange Syrup:

1. While the cake is baking, prepare the orange syrup. In a small saucepan, combine the orange juice and sugar. Bring to a simmer over medium heat, stirring occasionally, until the sugar is dissolved. Remove from heat and set aside.

3. Finish the Cake:

1. When the cake is done baking, remove it from the oven and place it on a wire rack.
2. Poke several holes in the top of the cake using a toothpick or skewer.
3. Slowly pour the warm orange syrup over the cake, allowing it to soak into the cake. Let the cake cool completely in the pan.

4. Prepare the Orange Glaze:

1. In a small bowl, whisk together the powdered sugar and 2-3 tablespoons of fresh orange juice until smooth and pourable. Add more juice if needed to achieve desired consistency.

5. Glaze the Cake:

1. Once the cake has cooled, remove it from the pan and place it on a serving plate or cake stand.
2. Drizzle the orange glaze over the top of the cake, allowing it to drip down the sides.
3. Sprinkle with orange zest, if desired, for garnish.
4. Slice and serve the moist and flavorful Gateau à l'Orange as a delightful dessert or treat with tea or coffee. Enjoy the citrusy goodness!

Flognarde

Ingredients:

- 3-4 ripe pears, peeled, cored, and sliced
- 3 large eggs
- 1/2 cup (100g) granulated sugar
- 1 cup (240ml) milk
- 1/2 cup (120ml) heavy cream
- 1/2 cup (60g) all-purpose flour
- 1/4 tsp salt
- 1 tsp vanilla extract
- Powdered sugar, for dusting

Instructions:

1. **Preheat Oven and Prepare Pan:**
    - Preheat your oven to 350°F (175°C). Grease a 9-inch (23cm) round baking dish or pie pan.
2. **Prepare the Pears:**
    - Peel, core, and slice the pears into thin slices. Arrange them evenly in the greased baking dish.
3. **Prepare the Batter:**
    - In a large bowl, whisk together the eggs and granulated sugar until pale and creamy.
4. **Add Milk and Cream:**
    - Gradually whisk in the milk and heavy cream until well combined.
5. **Mix in Flour and Flavorings:**
    - Add the flour, salt, and vanilla extract to the egg mixture. Whisk until the batter is smooth and no lumps remain.
6. **Pour Over Pears:**
    - Pour the batter over the arranged pear slices in the baking dish.
7. **Bake:**
    - Bake in the preheated oven for 35-40 minutes, or until the top is golden brown and a toothpick inserted into the center comes out clean.
8. **Cool and Serve:**
    - Remove from the oven and let the flognarde cool slightly. Dust with powdered sugar before serving.
9. **Serve Warm:**
    - Flognarde is traditionally served warm. Slice and enjoy this delicious French dessert with a scoop of vanilla ice cream or a dollop of whipped cream, if desired.

This recipe yields a comforting and rustic dessert that highlights the sweetness of pears in a custardy, cake-like texture.

Tarte aux Pruneaux

Ingredients:

- 1 sheet of store-bought or homemade pie crust
- 1 pound (450g) pitted prunes
- 1/2 cup (120ml) water
- 1/2 cup (100g) granulated sugar
- 1/2 tsp vanilla extract
- Zest of 1 lemon
- 1 tbsp rum (optional)
- 1 tbsp butter, cut into small pieces
- Powdered sugar, for dusting (optional)

Instructions:

1. **Prepare the Prunes:**
   - In a saucepan, combine the prunes, water, sugar, vanilla extract, lemon zest, and rum (if using). Bring to a simmer over medium heat.
2. **Cook the Prunes:**
   - Reduce the heat to low and let the prunes simmer gently for about 15-20 minutes, stirring occasionally, until the prunes are soft and the liquid has thickened slightly. Remove from heat and let cool slightly.
3. **Preheat Oven:**
   - Preheat your oven to 375°F (190°C).
4. **Prepare the Crust:**
   - Roll out the pie crust and line a 9-inch (23cm) tart pan with it. Trim any excess dough and prick the bottom of the crust with a fork.
5. **Fill the Tart:**
   - Spread the cooked prunes evenly over the tart crust. Arrange them in a single layer.
6. **Dot with Butter:**
   - Scatter small pieces of butter over the top of the prunes.
7. **Bake:**
   - Place the tart in the preheated oven and bake for 25-30 minutes, or until the crust is golden brown and the prunes are caramelized.
8. **Cool and Serve:**
   - Remove the tart from the oven and let it cool on a wire rack. Dust with powdered sugar before serving, if desired.
9. **Serve:**
   - Slice and serve the tarte aux pruneaux warm or at room temperature. It pairs wonderfully with a dollop of crème fraîche or a scoop of vanilla ice cream.

This classic French dessert showcases the sweetness and richness of prunes in a simple and delicious tart that is perfect for any occasion. Enjoy the rich flavors and aroma of this traditional French treat!

Gateau au Chocolat et aux Amandes

Ingredients:

- 200g dark chocolate, chopped
- 200g unsalted butter, softened
- 200g caster sugar
- 4 eggs
- 100g ground almonds
- 100g all-purpose flour
- 1 tsp baking powder
- 1/2 tsp salt
- 1 tsp vanilla extract
- Sliced almonds for decoration (optional)
- Icing sugar, for dusting (optional)

Instructions:

1. **Preparation:**
    - Preheat your oven to 180°C (350°F). Grease and line a 9-inch (23cm) round cake tin with parchment paper.
2. **Melt the Chocolate:**
    - In a heatproof bowl set over a pan of simmering water (double boiler method), melt the chopped chocolate until smooth. Set aside to cool slightly.
3. **Prepare the Batter:**
    - In a large mixing bowl, cream together the softened butter and caster sugar until pale and fluffy.
    - Beat in the eggs, one at a time, ensuring each egg is fully incorporated before adding the next.
    - Mix in the vanilla extract.
    - Fold in the melted chocolate gently until well combined.
    - In a separate bowl, combine the ground almonds, flour, baking powder, and salt.
    - Gradually add the dry ingredients to the wet mixture, folding gently until everything is combined and no streaks of flour remain.
4. **Bake the Cake:**
    - Pour the batter into the prepared cake tin and spread it out evenly.
    - If desired, sprinkle sliced almonds over the top of the cake batter for decoration.
    - Bake in the preheated oven for about 35-40 minutes, or until a skewer inserted into the center of the cake comes out clean.
5. **Cool and Serve:**
    - Remove the cake from the oven and let it cool in the tin for about 10 minutes.
    - Transfer the cake onto a wire rack to cool completely.
    - Once cooled, dust with icing sugar if desired.
6. **Serve:**
    - Slice and serve the chocolate almond cake on its own or with a dollop of whipped cream or a scoop of vanilla ice cream.

Enjoy this rich and decadent Chocolate and Almond Cake, perfect for any occasion!

Gateau Nantais

Ingredients:

For the cake:

- 200g (7 oz) unsalted butter, softened
- 200g (1 cup) granulated sugar
- 200g (1 1/2 cups) almond flour
- 100g (3/4 cup) all-purpose flour
- 4 large eggs
- 1/2 tsp almond extract
- Zest of 1 lemon
- Pinch of salt
- 1 tbsp dark rum (optional)

For the syrup:

- 100g (1/2 cup) granulated sugar
- 100ml (1/2 cup) water
- 2 tbsp dark rum

For the icing:

- 150g (1 1/4 cups) powdered sugar
- 2-3 tbsp dark rum
- Water, as needed

Instructions:

1. Preheat the oven and prepare the pan:

- Preheat your oven to 180°C (350°F). Butter and flour a 9-inch (23cm) round cake pan or line it with parchment paper.

2. Make the cake batter:

- In a mixing bowl, cream together the softened butter and granulated sugar until light and fluffy.
- Add the eggs one at a time, mixing well after each addition.
- Mix in the almond flour, all-purpose flour, almond extract, lemon zest, salt, and rum (if using) until smooth and well combined.

3. Bake the cake:

- Pour the batter into the prepared cake pan and smooth the top with a spatula.
- Bake in the preheated oven for about 30-35 minutes, or until a skewer inserted into the center of the cake comes out clean.

4. Prepare the syrup:

- While the cake is baking, prepare the syrup. In a small saucepan, combine the granulated sugar and water over medium heat.
- Stir until the sugar dissolves completely and the mixture comes to a gentle boil. Remove from heat and stir in the rum. Set aside to cool.

5. Soak the cake:

- Once the cake is baked and while it is still warm, poke holes all over the top with a skewer or toothpick.
- Pour the cooled syrup evenly over the warm cake, allowing it to absorb the syrup. Let the cake cool completely in the pan.

6. Make the icing:

- In a bowl, whisk together the powdered sugar and rum until smooth. Add water as needed, a little at a time, until you reach a thick but pourable consistency.

7. Ice the cake:

- Once the cake has cooled completely and absorbed the syrup, remove it from the pan onto a serving plate.
- Pour the icing over the top of the cake, allowing it to drip down the sides.

8. Serve:

- Slice and serve the Gateau Nantais at room temperature. It pairs well with coffee or tea and is perfect for dessert or a special occasion.

Enjoy this delicious and moist Gateau Nantais with its unique almond flavor and rum-infused syrup!

Gateu au Fromage Blanc

Ingredients:

For the cake:

- 500g (about 2 cups) fromage blanc (quark or cottage cheese can be substituted)
- 150g (3/4 cup) granulated sugar
- 4 large eggs, separated
- Zest of 1 lemon
- 1 tsp vanilla extract
- 60g (1/2 cup) all-purpose flour
- 30g (1/4 cup) cornstarch
- Pinch of salt

For the topping:

- 200g (about 1 cup) sour cream or crème fraîche
- 30g (2 tbsp) granulated sugar
- 1 tsp vanilla extract

Instructions:

1. Preheat the oven and prepare the pan:

- Preheat your oven to 180°C (350°F). Butter and flour a 9-inch (23cm) round cake pan or line it with parchment paper.

2. Prepare the cake batter:

- In a large bowl, mix together the fromage blanc and granulated sugar until smooth.
- Add the egg yolks one at a time, mixing well after each addition.
- Stir in the lemon zest and vanilla extract.
- Sift in the flour and cornstarch, and mix until just combined. Do not overmix.

3. Whip the egg whites:

- In a separate clean bowl, beat the egg whites with a pinch of salt until stiff peaks form.

4. Fold in the egg whites:

- Gently fold the whipped egg whites into the fromage blanc mixture in two additions, using a spatula. Be careful not to deflate the mixture.

5. Bake the cake:

- Pour the batter into the prepared cake pan and smooth the top with a spatula.
- Bake in the preheated oven for about 40-45 minutes, or until the cake is golden brown and set. A toothpick inserted into the center should come out clean.

6. Prepare the topping:

- While the cake is baking, prepare the topping. In a bowl, mix together the sour cream or crème fraîche, granulated sugar, and vanilla extract until smooth.

7. Finish the cake:

- Once the cake is baked, remove it from the oven and let it cool in the pan for about 10 minutes.
- Carefully spread the topping evenly over the warm cake.

8. Cool and serve:

- Allow the cake to cool completely in the pan before transferring it to a serving plate.
- Slice and serve the Gateau au Fromage Blanc at room temperature. It's delicious on its own or served with fresh berries or fruit compote.

Enjoy this light and creamy Gateau au Fromage Blanc as a delightful dessert or treat!

Tarte à la Rhubarbe

Ingredients:

For the crust:

- 200g (about 1 1/2 cups) all-purpose flour
- 100g (1/2 cup) cold unsalted butter, cut into small cubes
- 1 egg yolk
- 2-3 tbsp cold water
- Pinch of salt

For the filling:

- 500g (about 1 lb) fresh rhubarb, trimmed and cut into 1-inch pieces
- 150g (3/4 cup) granulated sugar
- 2 tbsp cornstarch
- 1 tsp vanilla extract
- Zest of 1 lemon
- 1 egg, beaten (for egg wash)

Instructions:

1. Prepare the crust:

- In a large bowl, combine the flour and salt. Add the cold butter cubes and rub them into the flour mixture with your fingertips until it resembles coarse breadcrumbs.
- Add the egg yolk and 2 tablespoons of cold water. Mix with a fork or your hands until the dough starts to come together. Add more water if needed, but do not overwork the dough.
- Shape the dough into a ball, flatten it into a disc, wrap it in plastic wrap, and refrigerate for at least 30 minutes.

2. Preheat the oven:

- Preheat your oven to 180°C (350°F).

3. Prepare the rhubarb filling:

- In a large bowl, toss the rhubarb pieces with sugar, cornstarch, vanilla extract, and lemon zest until well coated. Set aside to macerate for about 15-20 minutes.

4. Roll out the dough:

- On a lightly floured surface, roll out the chilled dough into a circle about 12 inches (30 cm) in diameter, and about 1/8 inch (3 mm) thick.
- Carefully transfer the rolled-out dough to a 9-inch (23 cm) tart pan with a removable bottom. Press the dough into the bottom and sides of the pan. Trim any excess dough hanging over the edges.

5. Assemble the tart:

- Arrange the macerated rhubarb pieces evenly over the prepared tart crust.

6. Bake the tart:

- Brush the edges of the tart crust with beaten egg to give it a shiny golden finish.
- Place the tart in the preheated oven and bake for about 40-45 minutes, or until the crust is golden brown and the rhubarb filling is bubbling and tender.

7. Cool and serve:

- Remove the tart from the oven and let it cool in the pan for about 10 minutes. Then carefully remove the tart from the pan and transfer it to a wire rack to cool completely.
- Serve the Tarte à la Rhubarbe at room temperature. Optionally, dust with powdered sugar before serving.

Enjoy this delicious and classic French Rhubarb Tart as a delightful dessert!

Gateau aux Framboises

Ingredients:

For the cake:

- 200g (1 1/2 cups) all-purpose flour
- 150g (3/4 cup) granulated sugar
- 150g (2/3 cup) unsalted butter, softened
- 3 large eggs
- 1 tsp vanilla extract
- 1 tsp baking powder
- 1/4 tsp salt
- 150g (1 1/2 cups) fresh raspberries

For the raspberry filling:

- 250g (2 cups) fresh raspberries
- 50g (1/4 cup) granulated sugar
- Juice of 1/2 lemon

For decoration (optional):

- Powdered sugar for dusting
- Fresh raspberries

Instructions:

1. Preheat the oven:

- Preheat your oven to 180°C (350°F). Grease and flour a 9-inch (23 cm) round cake pan or line it with parchment paper.

2. Prepare the raspberry filling:

- In a small saucepan, combine the 250g of raspberries, sugar, and lemon juice. Cook over medium heat, stirring occasionally, until the raspberries break down and the mixture thickens slightly (about 5-7 minutes). Remove from heat and let cool.

3. Make the cake batter:

- In a large bowl, cream together the softened butter and sugar until light and fluffy. Add the eggs one at a time, mixing well after each addition. Stir in the vanilla extract.
- In a separate bowl, whisk together the flour, baking powder, and salt. Gradually add the dry ingredients to the butter mixture, mixing until just combined.

4. Assemble the cake:

- Pour half of the cake batter into the prepared cake pan and spread it evenly. Spoon the cooled raspberry filling over the batter, leaving a small border around the edges.

- Scatter the remaining 150g of fresh raspberries evenly over the raspberry filling.
- Carefully spoon the remaining cake batter over the raspberries and spread it gently to cover them.

5. Bake the cake:

- Bake in the preheated oven for 35-40 minutes, or until a toothpick inserted into the center of the cake comes out clean.

6. Cool and decorate:

- Allow the cake to cool in the pan for 10 minutes before transferring it to a wire rack to cool completely.
- Dust with powdered sugar before serving, if desired. Garnish with fresh raspberries for an extra touch.

7. Serve and enjoy:

- Slice and serve the Gateau aux Framboises at room temperature. It's perfect for any occasion, especially with a cup of tea or coffee.

This raspberry cake is light, fruity, and perfect for showcasing fresh raspberries in season. Enjoy the delightful flavors of this Gateau aux Framboises!

Gateau au Citron

Ingredients:

For the cake:

- 200g (1 1/2 cups) all-purpose flour
- 200g (1 cup) granulated sugar
- 150g (2/3 cup) unsalted butter, softened
- 3 large eggs
- Zest of 2 lemons
- Juice of 1 lemon (about 4 tbsp)
- 1 tsp baking powder
- 1/4 tsp salt
- 120ml (1/2 cup) milk

For the lemon syrup:

- Juice of 1 lemon (about 4 tbsp)
- 50g (1/4 cup) granulated sugar

For the lemon glaze:

- Juice of 1 lemon (about 4 tbsp)
- 150g (1 1/4 cups) powdered sugar (icing sugar)

Instructions:

1. Preheat the oven:

- Preheat your oven to 180°C (350°F). Grease and flour a 9-inch (23 cm) round cake pan or line it with parchment paper.

2. Make the cake batter:

- In a large bowl, cream together the softened butter and granulated sugar until light and fluffy.
- Add the eggs one at a time, mixing well after each addition. Stir in the lemon zest and lemon juice.
- In a separate bowl, whisk together the flour, baking powder, and salt.
- Gradually add the dry ingredients to the butter mixture, alternating with the milk, beginning and ending with the flour mixture. Mix until just combined.

3. Bake the cake:

- Pour the batter into the prepared cake pan and spread it evenly.
- Bake in the preheated oven for 30-35 minutes, or until a toothpick inserted into the center of the cake comes out clean.

4. Make the lemon syrup:

- While the cake is baking, prepare the lemon syrup. In a small saucepan, heat the lemon juice and granulated sugar over medium heat until the sugar dissolves. Remove from heat and set aside.

5. Glaze the cake:

- Once the cake is baked, remove it from the oven and let it cool in the pan for about 10 minutes.
- While still warm, poke holes all over the top of the cake with a toothpick or skewer.
- Brush the warm lemon syrup over the top of the cake, allowing it to soak in.

6. Make the lemon glaze:

- In a small bowl, whisk together the lemon juice and powdered sugar until smooth and pourable. Adjust the consistency by adding more powdered sugar or lemon juice as needed.

7. Finish and serve:

- Once the cake has cooled completely, drizzle the lemon glaze over the top.
- Slice and serve the Gateau au Citron. It's wonderfully moist with a tangy lemon flavor, perfect for any occasion.

Enjoy this delightful Gateau au Citron with a cup of tea or coffee for a delightful treat!

Tarte aux Mirabelles

Ingredients:

For the pastry crust:

- 200g (1 2/3 cups) all-purpose flour
- 100g (1/2 cup) unsalted butter, cold and diced
- 50g (1/4 cup) granulated sugar
- 1 egg
- A pinch of salt

For the filling:

- 500g (about 1 lb) fresh mirabelle plums, pitted and halved
- 50g (1/4 cup) granulated sugar (adjust according to sweetness of plums)
- 1 tbsp cornstarch (corn flour)
- 1 tbsp lemon juice
- Zest of 1 lemon
- 1 tbsp apricot jam (for glazing)

Instructions:

1. Make the pastry crust:

- In a large mixing bowl, combine the flour, sugar, and salt. Add the cold diced butter.
- Using your fingertips or a pastry cutter, rub the butter into the flour mixture until it resembles coarse breadcrumbs.
- Add the egg and mix until the dough comes together. If it's too dry, add a tablespoon of cold water. Form the dough into a ball, flatten it into a disk, wrap in plastic wrap, and refrigerate for at least 30 minutes.

2. Prepare the filling:

- Preheat your oven to 180°C (350°F).
- In a bowl, toss the halved mirabelle plums with sugar, cornstarch, lemon juice, and lemon zest until well coated.

3. Roll out the pastry:

- On a lightly floured surface, roll out the chilled pastry dough into a circle about 30 cm (12 inches) in diameter and about 3-4 mm (1/8 inch) thick.
- Carefully transfer the rolled-out dough to a 24 cm (9 inch) tart pan with a removable bottom. Press the dough into the edges of the pan. Trim any excess dough hanging over the edge.

4. Assemble the tart:

- Arrange the coated mirabelle plum halves in a circular pattern over the pastry crust, starting from the outer edge and working your way inward.

- Once all the plums are arranged, gently fold the edges of the pastry over the plums, creating a rustic border.

5. Bake the tart:

- Place the tart on a baking sheet (to catch any drips) and bake in the preheated oven for 35-40 minutes, or until the crust is golden brown and the plums are tender.

6. Glaze the tart:

- While the tart is still warm, gently heat the apricot jam in a small saucepan until melted. Brush the melted apricot jam over the surface of the tart for a shiny glaze.

7. Serve:

- Allow the tart to cool slightly before slicing and serving. It can be enjoyed warm or at room temperature.

8. Enjoy:

- Serve the Tarte aux Mirabelles on its own or with a dollop of whipped cream or a scoop of vanilla ice cream. It's a delicious celebration of sweet, juicy mirabelle plums in a buttery pastry crust.

Far Breton

Ingredients:

- 200g (1 cup) pitted prunes (or other dried fruit like raisins)
- 125g (2/3 cup) granulated sugar
- 100g (3/4 cup) all-purpose flour
- A pinch of salt
- 4 large eggs
- 500ml (2 cups) whole milk
- 1 tsp vanilla extract
- Butter, for greasing

Instructions:

1. **Prepare the prunes:**
    - If using dried prunes, soak them in warm water for about 30 minutes to soften. Drain well and pat dry with paper towels. Cut larger prunes into smaller pieces if desired.
2. **Preheat the oven and prepare the baking dish:**
    - Preheat your oven to 180°C (350°F).
    - Generously butter a baking dish (traditionally a shallow round dish like a pie dish or a rectangular baking pan).
3. **Make the batter:**
    - In a large mixing bowl, whisk together the sugar, flour, and salt.
    - Add the eggs one at a time, whisking well after each addition, until smooth.
    - Gradually whisk in the milk and vanilla extract until the batter is smooth and well combined.
4. **Combine the prunes and batter:**
    - Arrange the prunes evenly in the buttered baking dish.
    - Pour the batter over the prunes, ensuring they are evenly distributed.
5. **Bake the Far Breton:**
    - Place the baking dish in the preheated oven and bake for about 45-50 minutes, or until the Far Breton is set and golden brown on top. It should have a slight wobble in the center but be firm around the edges.
6. **Cool and serve:**
    - Allow the Far Breton to cool slightly before serving. It can be served warm or at room temperature.
    - Optionally, sprinkle with powdered sugar before serving for a decorative touch.
7. **Enjoy:**
    - Serve slices of Far Breton on its own or with a dollop of whipped cream or a scoop of vanilla ice cream. It's a deliciously comforting dessert with a custardy texture and sweet bites of prunes throughout.

Far Breton is best enjoyed fresh on the day it's made, but leftovers can be stored in the refrigerator for a day or two and enjoyed chilled or reheated gently.

Gateau aux Marrons

Ingredients:

- 250g (9 oz) sweetened chestnut puree
- 100g (3.5 oz) unsalted butter, softened
- 100g (3.5 oz) granulated sugar
- 4 large eggs, separated
- 1 tsp vanilla extract
- 50g (1.8 oz) all-purpose flour
- 1 tsp baking powder
- Pinch of salt
- Powdered sugar, for dusting (optional)
- Whipped cream, for serving (optional)

Instructions:

1. **Prepare the Chestnut Puree:**
    - If your chestnut puree is too thick, you may need to thin it slightly with a little milk or cream.
2. **Preheat the Oven:**
    - Preheat your oven to 180°C (350°F). Grease and line an 8-inch (20 cm) round cake tin with parchment paper.
3. **Cream the Butter and Sugar:**
    - In a large bowl, cream together the softened butter and granulated sugar until light and fluffy.
4. **Add Egg Yolks and Vanilla:**
    - Separate the eggs, adding the yolks to the butter-sugar mixture one at a time, beating well after each addition. Add the vanilla extract and mix until combined.
5. **Incorporate the Chestnut Puree:**
    - Gradually add the chestnut puree to the butter-sugar mixture, beating until smooth and well combined.
6. **Combine Dry Ingredients:**
    - In a separate bowl, sift together the flour, baking powder, and salt.
7. **Fold in Dry Ingredients:**
    - Gently fold the dry ingredients into the chestnut mixture until just combined. Be careful not to overmix.
8. **Whip Egg Whites:**
    - In another clean bowl, whisk the egg whites until stiff peaks form.
9. **Fold in Egg Whites:**
    - Carefully fold the whipped egg whites into the batter in two additions, using a spatula. This will help to lighten the batter.
10. **Bake:**
    - Pour the batter into the prepared cake tin and smooth the top with a spatula.
    - Bake in the preheated oven for about 35-40 minutes, or until a toothpick inserted into the center comes out clean.
11. **Cool:**
    - Allow the cake to cool in the tin for 10 minutes before transferring to a wire rack to cool completely.

12. **Serve:**
    - Once cooled, dust the Gateau aux Marrons with powdered sugar if desired.
    - Serve slices of the cake on its own or with a dollop of whipped cream for an extra indulgent treat.

This Gateau aux Marrons is wonderfully moist and rich with the flavor of chestnuts, making it a perfect dessert for any occasion, especially during the fall and winter months.

Tarte au Chocolat

Ingredients:

For the Tart Shell:

- 200g (1 2/3 cups) all-purpose flour
- 100g (1/2 cup) unsalted butter, chilled and diced
- 50g (1/4 cup) granulated sugar
- 1 egg yolk
- 2-3 tablespoons cold water

For the Chocolate Filling:

- 200g (7 oz) dark chocolate (60-70% cocoa), chopped
- 200ml (3/4 cup + 2 tablespoons) heavy cream
- 50g (1/4 cup) granulated sugar
- 50g (1/4 cup) unsalted butter, diced
- 1 teaspoon vanilla extract
- Pinch of salt

Instructions:

1. Make the Tart Shell:

- In a large bowl, combine the flour and sugar. Add the chilled butter and rub it into the flour mixture using your fingertips until it resembles coarse breadcrumbs.
- Add the egg yolk and 2 tablespoons of cold water. Mix with a fork or your hands until the dough comes together. If the dough is too dry, add another tablespoon of cold water, a little at a time, until it forms a smooth ball.
- Flatten the dough into a disc, wrap it in plastic wrap, and refrigerate for at least 30 minutes.
- Preheat your oven to 180°C (350°F).
- On a lightly floured surface, roll out the dough into a circle about 12 inches (30 cm) in diameter. Carefully transfer the dough to a 9-inch (23 cm) tart pan with a removable bottom. Press the dough gently into the sides and bottom of the pan. Trim any excess dough hanging over the edges.
- Prick the bottom of the tart shell with a fork. Line the tart shell with parchment paper or aluminum foil and fill it with pie weights or dried beans.
- Bake the tart shell in the preheated oven for 15 minutes. Remove the parchment paper and weights, then bake for another 10 minutes or until the tart shell is golden brown. Remove from the oven and let it cool completely on a wire rack.

2. Make the Chocolate Filling:

- Place the chopped chocolate in a heatproof bowl.
- In a small saucepan, heat the heavy cream and sugar over medium heat until it just begins to simmer. Remove from heat immediately.
- Pour the hot cream mixture over the chopped chocolate. Let it sit for 1-2 minutes, then stir gently until the chocolate is completely melted and smooth.

- Add the diced butter, vanilla extract, and a pinch of salt to the chocolate mixture. Stir until the butter is melted and fully incorporated.

3. Assemble the Tart:

- Pour the chocolate filling into the cooled tart shell. Use a spatula to spread it evenly.
- Refrigerate the tart for at least 2 hours, or until the filling is set.
- Before serving, you can decorate the tart with whipped cream, chocolate shavings, or fresh berries if desired.

4. Serve:

- Slice and serve the Tarte au Chocolat chilled or at room temperature. Enjoy the rich, decadent chocolate flavor!

This Tarte au Chocolat is perfect for chocolate lovers and makes an elegant dessert for any special occasion or dinner party.

Quatre-Quarts

Ingredients:

- 250g (1 cup + 2 tablespoons) unsalted butter, softened, plus extra for greasing
- 250g (1 1/4 cups) granulated sugar
- 250g (2 cups) all-purpose flour
- 4 large eggs
- 1 teaspoon baking powder
- Pinch of salt
- 1 teaspoon vanilla extract (optional)

Instructions:

1. **Preheat Oven and Prepare Pan:**
   - Preheat your oven to 180°C (350°F). Grease and flour a 9-inch (23 cm) loaf pan or a round cake pan.
2. **Cream Butter and Sugar:**
   - In a large bowl, cream together the softened butter and sugar until light and fluffy. You can use a hand mixer or a stand mixer for this step.
3. **Add Eggs:**
   - Add the eggs one at a time, mixing well after each addition. Add a tablespoon of flour with each egg to prevent the mixture from curdling.
4. **Add Dry Ingredients:**
   - Sift the remaining flour, baking powder, and salt into the bowl with the butter mixture. Fold gently with a spatula or mixer on low speed until just combined. Do not overmix.
5. **Optional: Add Vanilla Extract:**
   - If using vanilla extract, stir it into the batter until evenly distributed.
6. **Bake:**
   - Pour the batter into the prepared pan and smooth the top with a spatula. Bake in the preheated oven for 45-55 minutes, or until a toothpick inserted into the center comes out clean.
7. **Cool:**
   - Remove the cake from the oven and let it cool in the pan for 10 minutes. Then, transfer the cake to a wire rack to cool completely.
8. **Serve:**
   - Once cooled, slice and serve the Quatre-Quarts plain or with a dusting of powdered sugar. It's also delicious with a spread of jam or fresh fruit.

Quatre-Quarts is a versatile cake that can be enjoyed for breakfast, as a snack, or as a dessert. Its name, which means "four quarters" in French, refers to the equal proportions of its four main ingredients: butter, sugar, flour, and eggs. Enjoy this simple and delightful French treat!

Gateau au Miel

Ingredients:

- 200g (1 1/4 cups) all-purpose flour
- 100g (1/2 cup) granulated sugar
- 3 large eggs
- 100g (1/2 cup) unsalted butter, melted
- 100g (1/3 cup) honey
- 1 tsp baking powder
- 1/2 tsp baking soda
- Pinch of salt
- 1/2 tsp ground cinnamon
- 1/4 tsp ground nutmeg (optional)
- 1/4 tsp ground cloves (optional)
- Zest of 1 lemon
- 60ml (1/4 cup) milk

Instructions:

1. **Preheat Oven and Prepare Pan:**
   - Preheat your oven to 180°C (350°F). Grease and flour a 9-inch (23 cm) round cake pan or a similar-sized loaf pan.
2. **Mix Dry Ingredients:**
   - In a bowl, sift together the flour, baking powder, baking soda, salt, cinnamon, and optional spices (nutmeg and cloves). Set aside.
3. **Mix Wet Ingredients:**
   - In a separate large bowl, whisk together the eggs and sugar until pale and fluffy. Add the melted butter, honey, lemon zest, and milk. Mix until well combined.
4. **Combine Wet and Dry Ingredients:**
   - Gradually add the dry ingredients to the wet ingredients, mixing gently until just combined. Be careful not to overmix.
5. **Bake:**
   - Pour the batter into the prepared pan and smooth the top with a spatula. Bake in the preheated oven for 30-35 minutes, or until a toothpick inserted into the center comes out clean.
6. **Cool:**
   - Remove the cake from the oven and let it cool in the pan for 10 minutes. Then, transfer the cake to a wire rack to cool completely.
7. **Serve:**
   - Once cooled, slice and serve the Gateau au Miel. It's delicious on its own or with a dollop of whipped cream, a drizzle of honey, or a sprinkle of powdered sugar.

Gateau au Miel is perfect for tea time or as a simple dessert. The honey adds a lovely sweetness and depth of flavor, making it a delightful treat for honey lovers. Enjoy!

Tarte aux Myrtilles

Ingredients:

For the Pastry:

- 200g (1 1/2 cups) all-purpose flour
- 100g (1/2 cup) unsalted butter, cold and diced
- 50g (1/4 cup) granulated sugar
- 1 egg yolk
- 2-3 tablespoons cold water

For the Filling:

- 500g (about 3 cups) fresh blueberries
- 100g (1/2 cup) granulated sugar
- 2 tablespoons cornstarch
- Juice and zest of 1 lemon

For Glaze (Optional):

- 2 tablespoons apricot jam
- 1 tablespoon water

Instructions:

1. **Make the Pastry:**
    - In a large bowl, combine the flour and sugar. Add the cold diced butter and rub it into the flour mixture using your fingertips until it resembles breadcrumbs.
    - Add the egg yolk and 2 tablespoons of cold water. Mix with a fork or your hands until the dough comes together. If needed, add more water, 1 tablespoon at a time.
    - Shape the dough into a ball, wrap it in plastic wrap, and refrigerate for at least 30 minutes.
2. **Prepare the Filling:**
    - In a small bowl, mix together the sugar and cornstarch.
    - In a large bowl, gently toss the blueberries with the sugar mixture, lemon juice, and lemon zest until evenly coated. Set aside.
3. **Assemble the Tart:**
    - Preheat your oven to 180°C (350°F).
    - On a lightly floured surface, roll out the chilled pastry dough into a circle about 12 inches (30 cm) in diameter and about 1/4 inch (0.5 cm) thick.
    - Carefully transfer the rolled-out dough to a 9-inch (23 cm) tart pan with a removable bottom. Press the dough into the bottom and sides of the pan, trimming any excess dough.
4. **Add the Filling:**
    - Pour the blueberry filling into the prepared pastry shell, spreading it out evenly.
5. **Bake the Tart:**
    - Place the tart on a baking sheet (to catch any drips) and bake in the preheated oven for 35-40 minutes, or until the pastry is golden brown and the blueberries are bubbling.

6. **Optional Glaze:**
    - While the tart is baking, heat the apricot jam and water in a small saucepan over medium heat until melted and smooth. Strain through a fine sieve to remove any solids.
7. **Finish the Tart:**
    - Remove the tart from the oven and let it cool on a wire rack for at least 15 minutes.
    - If using the glaze, brush it over the warm tart to give it a shiny finish.
    - Allow the tart to cool completely before slicing and serving.

Enjoy this delicious Tarte aux Myrtilles with a dollop of whipped cream or a scoop of vanilla ice cream. It's perfect for showcasing fresh blueberries in a delightful French pastry!

Gateau aux Abricots

Ingredients:

For the Cake:

- 200g (1 1/2 cups) all-purpose flour
- 150g (3/4 cup) granulated sugar
- 100g (1/2 cup) unsalted butter, softened
- 3 large eggs
- 1 teaspoon baking powder
- 1/4 teaspoon salt
- 1 teaspoon vanilla extract
- Zest of 1 lemon
- 1/2 cup milk

For the Topping:

- 8-10 fresh apricots, halved and pitted
- 2 tablespoons granulated sugar
- 1 tablespoon apricot jam, for glaze

Instructions:

1. **Prepare the Apricots:**
    - Preheat your oven to 180°C (350°F). Grease a 9-inch (23 cm) round cake pan and line the bottom with parchment paper.
    - Wash the apricots, cut them in half, and remove the pits.
2. **Make the Cake Batter:**
    - In a medium bowl, whisk together the flour, baking powder, and salt. Set aside.
    - In a large bowl, cream together the softened butter and sugar until light and fluffy.
    - Add the eggs one at a time, beating well after each addition. Mix in the vanilla extract and lemon zest.
    - Gradually add the flour mixture to the butter mixture, alternating with the milk, beginning and ending with the flour mixture. Mix until just combined.
3. **Assemble the Cake:**
    - Pour the cake batter into the prepared cake pan and smooth the top with a spatula.
    - Arrange the apricot halves, cut side up, on top of the batter. Sprinkle the apricots evenly with 2 tablespoons of granulated sugar.
4. **Bake the Cake:**
    - Bake in the preheated oven for 35-40 minutes, or until the cake is golden brown and a toothpick inserted into the center comes out clean.
5. **Glaze the Cake:**
    - While the cake is still warm, heat the apricot jam in a small saucepan over low heat until melted and smooth.
    - Brush the warm apricot jam over the top of the cake to give it a shiny glaze.
6. **Serve:**
    - Allow the cake to cool in the pan for 10 minutes, then carefully remove it from the pan and transfer it to a wire rack to cool completely.

- Slice and serve the Gateau aux Abricots at room temperature. Enjoy!

This Gateau aux Abricots is perfect for showcasing the natural sweetness of fresh apricots in a simple and delightful French cake.

Gateau au Beurre

Ingredients:

- 250g (2 cups) all-purpose flour
- 200g (1 cup) granulated sugar
- 200g (1 cup) unsalted butter, softened
- 4 large eggs
- 1 teaspoon vanilla extract
- 1/2 teaspoon baking powder
- Pinch of salt

Instructions:

1. **Prepare the Oven and Pan:**
   - Preheat your oven to 180°C (350°F). Grease and flour a 9-inch (23 cm) round cake pan or line it with parchment paper.
2. **Mix the Dry Ingredients:**
   - In a medium bowl, whisk together the flour, baking powder, and salt. Set aside.
3. **Cream the Butter and Sugar:**
   - In a large bowl, using an electric mixer or stand mixer fitted with the paddle attachment, cream together the softened butter and granulated sugar until light and fluffy.
4. **Incorporate Eggs and Vanilla:**
   - Add the eggs one at a time, beating well after each addition. Mix in the vanilla extract until combined.
5. **Combine Wet and Dry Ingredients:**
   - Gradually add the flour mixture to the butter mixture, mixing on low speed until just combined. Scrape down the sides of the bowl as needed, ensuring all ingredients are well incorporated.
6. **Bake the Cake:**
   - Pour the batter into the prepared cake pan and smooth the top with a spatula.
   - Bake in the preheated oven for 35-40 minutes, or until the cake is golden brown and a toothpick inserted into the center comes out clean.
7. **Cool and Serve:**
   - Allow the cake to cool in the pan for 10 minutes before transferring it to a wire rack to cool completely.
8. **Optional: Dust with Powdered Sugar:**
   - Once cooled, dust the Gateau au Beurre with powdered sugar before serving for a decorative touch.
9. **Serve:**
   - Slice and serve the Gateau au Beurre on its own or with a dollop of whipped cream, fresh berries, or your favorite topping.

Enjoy this deliciously buttery French cake, perfect for any occasion!

Tarte aux Figues

Ingredients:

For the Tart Crust:

- 200g (1 1/2 cups) all-purpose flour
- 100g (1/2 cup) cold unsalted butter, diced
- 50g (1/4 cup) granulated sugar
- 1 egg
- Pinch of salt

For the Fig Filling:

- 500g (about 1 lb) fresh figs, washed and stemmed
- 100g (1/2 cup) granulated sugar
- 1 tablespoon lemon juice
- 1 teaspoon vanilla extract

Optional Glaze:

- 2 tablespoons apricot jam or fig jam, warmed

Instructions:

1. **Prepare the Tart Crust:**
   - In a large mixing bowl, combine the flour, sugar, and salt.
   - Add the cold diced butter and rub it into the flour mixture with your fingertips until it resembles breadcrumbs.
   - Add the egg and mix until the dough comes together. If needed, add a tablespoon of cold water to bring it together into a smooth ball.
   - Wrap the dough in plastic wrap and refrigerate for at least 30 minutes.
2. **Prepare the Fig Filling:**
   - Preheat your oven to 180°C (350°F).
   - Slice the figs into quarters or thick slices, depending on their size.
   - In a bowl, gently toss the figs with sugar, lemon juice, and vanilla extract until evenly coated.
3. **Assemble the Tart:**
   - On a lightly floured surface, roll out the chilled tart dough into a circle large enough to fit your tart pan (about 9-10 inches in diameter).
   - Carefully transfer the dough to your tart pan, pressing it gently into the bottom and up the sides. Trim any excess dough from the edges.
   - Arrange the prepared fig slices in an overlapping pattern on top of the tart crust.
4. **Bake the Tart:**
   - Place the tart in the preheated oven and bake for 30-35 minutes, or until the crust is golden brown and the figs are tender.
5. **Optional Glaze:**
   - If desired, warm the apricot or fig jam in a small saucepan until it becomes liquid. Brush the warm glaze over the figs to give them a shiny finish.

6. **Serve:**
    - Allow the tart to cool slightly before serving. It can be served warm or at room temperature.
    - Optionally, serve with a dollop of whipped cream, a scoop of vanilla ice cream, or a sprinkle of powdered sugar.

Enjoy this elegant Tarte aux Figues as a delightful dessert showcasing the natural sweetness of fresh figs!